According to Plan

The story of God and his people

Noel E. Weiss

OPENBOOK
P U B L I S H E R S
Adelaide, South Australia

ACCORDING TO PLAN

Editorial Committee: P.W. Boesch, Everard Leske, G.W. Matuschka, Dr. V.C. Pfitzner, D.A. Schubert, D.T. Strelan, N.E. Weiss, J.E. Zweck.

Graphic Design and Layout: Graeme Cogdell.

The use of Scripture quotations from the *Revised Standard Version*, copyright 1952, 1971 by the Division of Christian Education, National Council of Churches USA, from the *Good News Bible — Today's English Version*, copyright 1976 by the American Bible Society, or from the *Holy Bible — New International Version*, copyright 1978 by the New York International Bible Society, is gratefully acknowledged.

National Library of Australia
Cataloguing-in-Publication data

Weiss, Noel E. (Noel Eric), 1928–
  According to plan.

  Includes index.
  ISBN 0 85910 315 3.

  1. Bible — Juvenile literature. I. Title.
220

First printing December 1984

00 99 98   22 21 20

Printed and published by
Openbook Publishers,
205 Halifax Street, Adelaide, South Australia

1535-95

CONTENTS

FOREWORD

God has a plan — a wonderful plan for the world and its people. How God put this plan into action, and carried it out, is the greatest story ever told. It is the story told in the Bible.

According to Plan has been written to help you understand this story of God and his people, and to help you learn about God's great plan. In this book you will discover more and more about:

- God's wonderful love — how God planned good things for his people, and patiently worked out his plan despite their sin and weakness;
- God's mighty power and wisdom — how God has been continually at work to help and guide his people;
- God's astonishing way of saving the world — how God himself came to earth to carry out his promises;
- God's place for us in his plan — how still today God brings his love to us and makes us his people.

We hope that you will be excited and glad to discover how God does everything to make his plan come true.

A Book to Help You Grow

In this book you will get an overview of the Bible story and its main themes. It will help you to see the main points in the story of God and his people, and how they all fit together in God's plan. You can explore the Bible to see more clearly how God carried out his plan, stage by stage. You can join in discussing what God is doing, and talk about what this means for God's people today.

This book contains a lot of material — more than you can use. Your teacher will guide you as to what activities you should do. In each chapter, a special section also helps your family to join in what you are doing; we hope you will **share at home** what you are learning about God's plan.

Be glad that you are one of God's people, and that you are included in his plans! Through your study, may you grow in your love for God and his Word, and become ever more sure that God truly cares for you and will carry out all his promises —

ACCORDING TO PLAN!

Noel E. Weiss

God's amazing plan

Have you ever watched a team of builders at work putting up a new school or shopping centre? They build a wall here, and another wall over there. Here they put a door; there they put a window. At first, it seems to us like a hopeless jumble. But the builders seem to know exactly what to do.

How do the builders know where to put all the walls and doors and windows? They have a **plan**. An architect has drawn up a plan for the building, and they simply follow it step by step.

If we study the architect's drawings, we understand much better just what the builders are doing, and what the building will look like when it is finished.

It makes all the difference when you can see the plan.

GOD HAS A PLAN

It's like that, too, with our life in this world. Sometimes it is hard to understand just what is going on in the world and in our life. Many things just don't make sense. We wonder how it will all work out in the end.

But there is a plan for our world — the greatest anyone has ever made. This is **God's plan**, which he drew up even before the world began. Step by step, God has been putting his plan into action for thousands of years. He is still carrying it out right now in our lives. And he will complete the final details when this world comes to an end.

By getting to know this plan, we can understand better the things that have happened and are still happening. We can find the answers to many questions about ourselves and our lives.

WE CAN SEE GOD'S PLAN

God has put his plan on display in the Bible. When we read the stories of the Bible, we can trace the details and see how they all fit together.

In this Bible history course, you will learn what God's plan is and how he has been carrying it out. But you will also discover how again and again people go against what God intends. Often they seem to mess things up so badly that it looks impossible for God's plan to work out.

You may be a bit puzzled at times by the way God acts. He does strange things as he follows his great plan. You will certainly be amazed at how patient and loving God is with people — even when they try to follow their own plans instead of his.

PEOPLE IN GOD'S PLAN

You will meet all sorts of people who come into God's plan — some good, some not so good. It may shock you to learn just how bad some of the people were whom God fitted into his grand scheme.

Above all, you will get to meet the one special Person whom God used to make sure that his plan worked out just the way he wanted. You will see that, all along, God's plan depends on this Person. In a most amazing way, he makes happen the good and wonderful things God has in mind.

As you learn about God's amazing plan, you may find yourself thinking: 'I wish God would include me in what he is doing!'

Do you know what? You **are** in God's plan. You always have been, and you always will be.

As you study the details of God's plan, the important question for you to ask is: 'What does this mean for me?'

STAGES IN GOD'S PLAN

In this study you will learn that there are three main stages in God's plan:

Stage I   — from the beginning of the world to the coming of Jesus

Stage II   — the coming of Jesus to save all people

Stage III — from the coming of Jesus to the end of the world

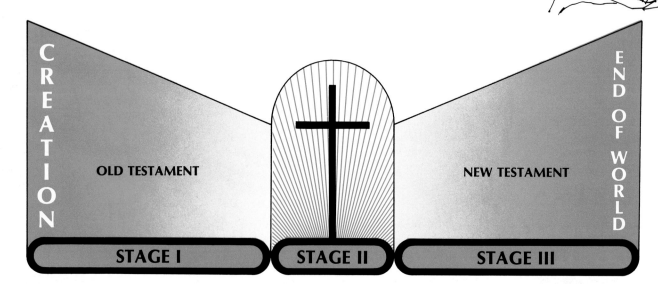

CREATION

OLD TESTAMENT

NEW TESTAMENT

END OF WORLD

STAGE I   STAGE II   STAGE III

BIBLE SEARCH
READ PSALM 78:1–7.

What story is the psalm-writer telling? Why does he want to tell this story?

From the rest of the psalm, find an example of the glorious deeds of God that the psalm-writer wants to tell about.

6

THE BOOK OF GOD'S PLAN

God has not kept his amazing plan a secret; he has told us about it in the Bible. The Bible (or Holy Scripture) is God's book; it is God's Word. God inspired men to write the Scriptures. This means that God led them to write down just what he wanted.

Down through the centuries, the Old Testament writers wrote about the great things God was doing to carry out his plan. Sometimes God also told them to write about what was going to happen in the future. They especially wrote about the promise that a Saviour would come.

The Old Testament writers did not always understand all the details about God's plan as they happened. But when Jesus came, he explained God's will to us. He showed how all the great and wonderful things God had done and promised fitted into his masterplan.

The New Testament writers wrote about what Jesus did and what Jesus taught. The Holy Spirit led them to understand clearly that, through Jesus, God's plan has been carried out, and will work out until the end of the world.

When we read the Bible, we look back and see God following his plan. We also learn from the Bible how we are included in God's amazing plan.

BIBLE SEARCH
READ HEBREWS 1:1,2.
Through whom did God speak in the old days?

Talk about some of the ways in which God spoke in Old Testament times.

Through whom has God spoken in New Testament times?

KEY BIBLE PASSAGE   2 TIMOTHY 3:14–17
The Bible is God's Word, so we can believe it is true. The Bible shows us God's plan to save us through Jesus.

Why is the Bible God's Word, even though it was written by men? For what purposes has God given us the Bible?

LET'S DO SOME THINKING

1. Can you pinpoint events in the Bible that happened just the way God planned them? Can you also think of examples of how people went against God's plan?

2. Why do you think the Bible tells us not only the **good** things people did, but also the **bad** things?

3. Can you name other people besides Jesus whom God used to carry out his plan for the world?

4. How does it help us to know that, from the beginning to the end of the world, God is at work carrying out his amazing plan?

WORSHIP

Dear Father in heaven, we thank you for giving us the Holy Scriptures which tell us of your great and loving plan for us and for all people. Give us your Holy Spirit as we study your Word, so that we may believe what you tell us, and be happy to live in your love, through Jesus Christ, our Lord. Amen.

WITH YOUR FAMILY

Find out from your parents what they know about your family's history. Talk about examples of how God has been at work in the story of your family. Read Romans 8:28 and talk about what this means for your family.

MORE THINGS TO DO

1. Prepare a time-line of Bible history for display in the classroom. Details in the time-line can be filled in as you study the main people and events of the Old Testament. With your teacher, decide now on the main stages for the time-line.

2. Interview some older people in your congregation, and talk to them about what the Bible means to them and how they use it. Report to the class.

3. Read Psalm 105. List the chief events which the writer remembers.

4. Prepare a large chart of the books of the Old Testament. Use different colours for the different kinds of books. Begin a program for learning the names of the Old Testament books.

5. Find out what is meant by a 'Jesse Tree'. Draw one, placing on it some of the most important Old Testament people God used in his plan of salvation.

6. Work out a plan for reading selections from the Old Testament regularly during this course.

PART ONE: THE OLD TESTAMENT

We can trace the details of Stage 1 of God's masterplan in the first part of the Bible, called the 'Old Testament'.

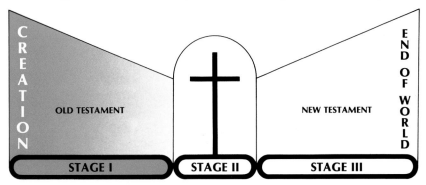

The stories in the Old Testament tell us how:

● God creates human beings to live with him in perfect happiness;

● human beings fall into sin, so that God's plan becomes his **saving plan**;

● God chooses one nation as the people through whom he will carry out his plan to save the world;

● God makes a covenant (**Testament** or agreement) with this nation that he will be their God and will keep them as his people;

● according to God's plan, **one Person** will come from the chosen nation to be the Saviour of all people.

THIS PROMISE OF A SAVIOUR IS THE KEY TO UNDERSTANDING GOD'S PLAN

THE OLD TESTAMENT

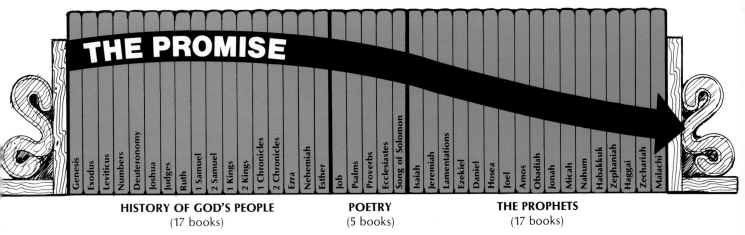

HISTORY OF GOD'S PEOPLE (17 books)   POETRY (5 books)   THE PROPHETS (17 books)

The Old Testament was written in the Hebrew language, over a period of about one thousand years (1400–400 BC) by men whom God chose and inspired.

There are three kinds of writings in the thirty-nine books of the Old Testament: books of history, books of poetry, and books of prophecy.

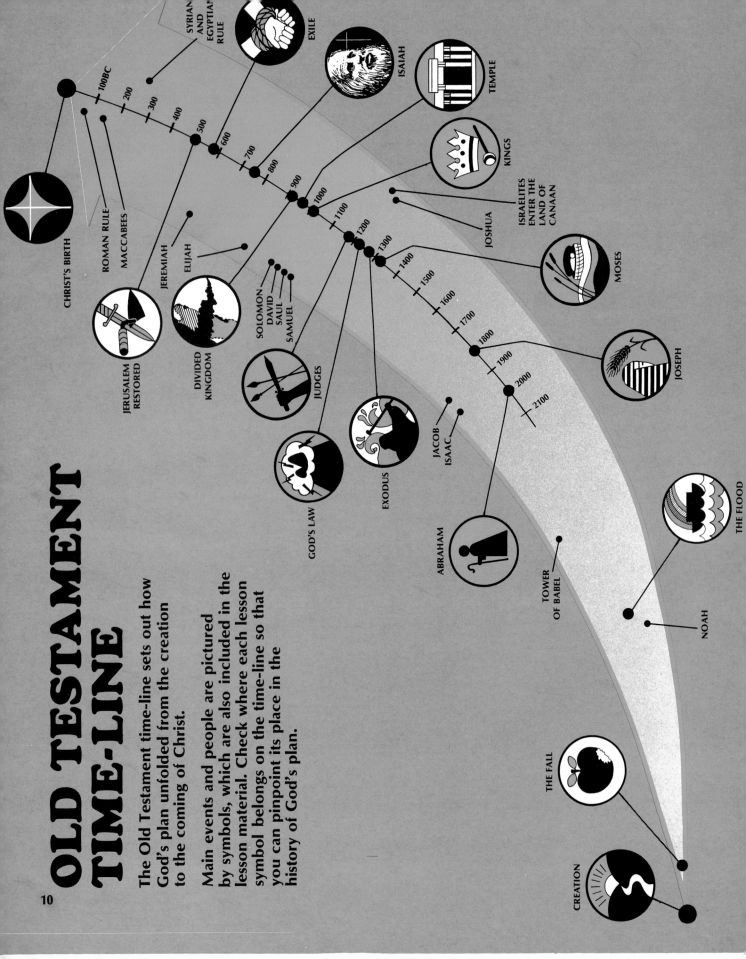

OLD TESTAMENT TIME-LINE

The Old Testament time-line sets out how God's plan unfolded from the creation to the coming of Christ.

Main events and people are pictured by symbols, which are also included in the lesson material. Check where each lesson symbol belongs on the time-line so that you can pinpoint its place in the history of God's plan.

SYRIAN AND EGYPTIAN RULE

EXILE

ISAIAH

TEMPLE

KINGS

ISRAELITES ENTER THE LAND OF CANAAN

JOSHUA

MOSES

JOSEPH

100BC
200
300
400
500
600
700
800
900
1000
1100
1200
1300
1400
1500
1600
1700
1800
1900
2000
2100

CHRIST'S BIRTH

ROMAN RULE

MACCABEES

JEREMIAH

ELIJAH

SOLOMON
DAVID
SAUL
SAMUEL

JERUSALEM RESTORED

DIVIDED KINGDOM

JUDGES

GOD'S LAW

EXODUS

JACOB
ISAAC

ABRAHAM

TOWER OF BABEL

NOAH

THE FLOOD

THE FALL

CREATION

In the beginning

We live on a very beautiful planet in a marvellous universe. Have you ever wondered: 'Where does this all come from? How did it all begin?' Perhaps you have also asked: 'Why does the world exist? Why are we here?'
What are some of the answers people give to these questions?

The Bible helps us to look back and see God beginning his plan by creating all things.

In the beginning
there was God.
No one else, nothing else.
Only God.
    In the beginning God created.
Out of nothing, by his Word
he made matter and formed
the universe.
God turned his attention to one little planet —
Earth.
He spoke,
and life came on Earth,
on the land, in the sea, in the air.
God created the heavens and the earth,
a beautiful home,
in the beginning.
    In the beginning God created
beings like himself
to live on Earth —
beautiful, good beings, who could
think and feel
and love.
    God created human beings whom he could love,
and who could love him
and one another.
He wanted them to live with him,
perfect and happy for ever.
    This was God's plan
in the beginning.

THE STORIES OF CREATION

   In the first two chapters of the Bible, God tells us about his work as the Creator.
There are really two stories here:

● The first story (Genesis 1:1–2:3) tells how God made the universe and filled the earth with living things in six days.

● The second story (Genesis 2:4–24) tells us more about how God made the first man and woman, and gave them a special place in which to live.

**God created light.
He separated light from darkness.
He made day and night.**

**God separated the water above
from the water below the
firmament.
He made the sky.**

**God separated the water from the
dry land. He made the land and
the sea, and plants to grow on the
land.**

**BIBLE SEARCH
READ GENESIS 1:1-12** (days 1,2,3).
Talk about how God created an
orderly world from chaos.
READ GENESIS 1:14-25 (days 4,5,6).
How are the first three days connected to the next
three? (See the matching symbols drawn in the
diagrams above.)
Why did God make the sun and moon? the fish and
birds? the animals?

HOW GOD CREATED HUMAN BEINGS

God had filled his beautiful earth with living
creatures of many kinds: animals, birds, fish,
insects, reptiles. But his plan was to have one living
creature who would be superior to all others. The
climax of God's creation would be an intelligent
being who could know his Creator, love him, and
communicate with him. God wanted a special
being who could appreciate the beautiful world
and take care of it as his servant.

So, from the earth's soil God formed a human body. He breathed life
into that body. The first man, Adam, now began life on earth perfect in
every way, just like his Maker. He was created in God's image, or likeness.

God gave Adam a beautiful garden, called 'Eden', as his home. He told
Adam to look after the garden and to be in charge of all the creatures on
earth.

God saw that Adam needed someone like himself as a companion and
helper. While Adam was asleep, God took one of Adam's ribs and formed
a woman, Eve. Adam was happy to have a special partner whom he could
love, and with whom he could share God's creation.

God blessed Adam and Eve with the ability to have children, so that the
earth could be populated by human beings. God's plan was that the
human race should live for ever in perfect happiness, and in peace with
God and with one another.

12

At first, the earth was just a shapeless mass of matter.
Everything was completely dark. The earth was covered with water, and there was no sky.
Then, in six days God formed the earth and prepared the earth for life. He also filled the earth with living creatures.

4♦ God made the sun and moon to rule over the day and night. He made the stars also.

5• God made the fish and other creatures to live in the sea, and birds to fly in the sky.

6▲ God made animals of every kind to live on the dry land. Finally, God made Adam and Eve.

7 God rested on the seventh day. This means, he had finished his work of creating. God saw that everything he had made was very good. Everything was going according to his plan.

BIBLE SEARCH

READ GENESIS 2:15-17.

What work did Adam have to do in the garden?   How do you think Adam felt about his work?

Why did Adam not have to worry about his daily needs?

What did God not allow Adam to do? Why do you think God put this one limit on Adam's freedom?

THE MAIN POINTS

● The world and all living creatures did not come into existence by accident; they were created by God according to his plan.

● God showed his almighty power by creating people who could live in a happy and loving relationship with him and with one another.

● All that God created was very good.

KEY BIBLE PASSAGE   GENESIS 1:26-31

Why did God make the first people?

How did God bless Adam and Eve?

Give examples of how human beings are in control of the earth.

FOR US TODAY

1. We ask many questions about how and why the world began. What is the most important answer to such questions that God gives us in the Bible? What difference does it make to your life when you 'believe in God the Father almighty, Maker of heaven and earth'?
Read Psalm 139:13–17.

2. The God who made all things is the God we worship: Father, Son, and Holy Spirit. From the following Bible passages, find out how each of the three persons of God was involved in the work of creation:
   - The Father   : Malachi 2:10
   - The Son   : John 1:1,2; Colossians 1:15–17
   - The Holy Spirit : Genesis 1:2; Job 33:4.

3. The story of creation tells of the many good things God planned in order to make human beings happy. Which of these good things can we still enjoy today? Can we enjoy them as much as Adam and Eve did?

Read responsively from Psalm 8:

O LORD, our Lord :
   Your greatness is seen in all the world!
You made man inferior only to yourself :
   You crowned him with glory and honour.
You appointed him ruler over everything you made :
   You placed him over all creation.

O LORD, our Lord :
   Your greatness is seen in all the world!

Scripture reference: Genesis 1,2.

14

 WITH YOUR FAMILY

1. Perhaps there is a picture of a nature scene in your home (for example, on a calendar). Use this as a background for a family devotion.

Read Psalm 136:1–9. Members of the family can share how they feel about the wonder and beauty of creation. Conclude with a prayer thanking God for the beautiful world he has given us.

2. Talk with your family about ways in which we can take good care of the earth.

MORE TO DO

1. Prepare posters illustrating the seven days of creation.

2. Read Job 38:1–15. How is the story of creation told here? Compare this with Genesis 1.

3. When God made the earth he saw that it was 'very good'. Share an experience you have had of the beauty of nature.

4. Volunteer to clean the grounds of the church, or to help at the home of an elderly person in the congregation.

5. Talk about some modern ideas of how life began on earth. Compare these ideas with the stories in Genesis.

Psalm 100:3-4

Things go wrong

> When you read the newspapers or watch the television news, what picture do you get of our world and the people in it?

What do you think Adam and Eve would say about our world if they could come back? Perhaps they would say: 'That's not what God planned'. There would be something else they could tell us. They could explain what has gone wrong with our world.

A SIMPLE TEST

When God made Adam and Eve like himself, he gave them a will of their own. They were not robots, for they could make decisions for themselves. So they could choose to obey or to disobey God.

There was one thing God had said they were not allowed to do. In the middle of the garden he placed a tree called 'the tree of knowledge of good and evil'. 'You may eat any other fruit', God said, 'but you must not eat the fruit from this tree. If you disobey me, you will die.'

This was a test for Adam and Eve. They had no trouble with this simple test until a cunning snake began talking to Eve. (The Bible tells us in other places that Satan, the devil, was the cause of this temptation.) The snake tried to make Eve doubt God's Word. 'You won't die if you eat that fruit', he lied; 'God just doesn't want you to be as wise as he is, knowing good and evil.'

The idea of being as wise as God appealed to Eve. The fruit looked good, too. So she took some of the fruit and ate it. Then she gave some to Adam, and he ate it also. Adam and Eve had disobeyed God's command.

This was the first sin. And it had terrible consequences. Now everything was spoilt. The man and woman became ashamed of their naked bodies, and covered themselves with fig-leaves. They felt afraid to face God. When he wanted to talk to them, they hid from him because they were guilty. When God questioned them about what they had done, they tried to make excuses and to pass off the blame.

Worse was to follow. God told them their sin had brought a curse on the earth. Now they would have to work hard to get their food. Now child-bearing would bring Eve pain. Now Adam and Eve could no longer live with God in perfect happiness, as he had planned, and they were sent from the safety of the garden. And, just as God had warned them, they would die.

15

Sin brought death into the world. Adam and Eve's children were born like them — sinful human beings, who were not fit to live with God for ever. One of their sons, Cain, became jealous of his brother, Abel, and murdered him.

GOD SHOWS HIS LOVE

Even though Adam and Eve had acted against God's plan, he still loved them. He told them that one day evil would be overcome. When he pronounced his punishment on the snake, God promised:

'He [the seed of the woman] **shall bruise your head, and you shall bruise his heel'** (Genesis 3:15).

So God gave the human race hope for the future. Even though they had become sinful, God did not give up his great plan.

BIBLE SEARCH

READ GENESIS 3:12,13,14–19.

Find out:

Whom did Adam and Eve blame for their fall into sin? Why didn't they own up?

Talk about God's punishment of the snake and of the man and woman.

Why did God not simply destroy his disobedient creatures?

GOD'S GREAT RESCUE

As Adam and Eve's family grew, people began to spread over the earth. They showed that they had inherited the sinfulness of the first parents by acts of great violence and wickedness. The human race had become just the opposite of what God had planned.

What would God do now? He decided to destroy the earth with a flood and to make a new start all over again.

Of all the people in the world, only one man and his family feared and trusted God. God told this man, Noah, to build an ark in which he would be safe when the flood came. Noah obeyed God. When the flood destroyed all other living creatures, God saved Noah and his family, together with pairs of all animals which Noah took with him into the ark.

God sent the great flood to cleanse the world, and to save Noah and his family from its wickedness. Through them he would still carry out his great plan.

God's loving care brought new life for the world after the flood. When Noah came out of the ark, he built an altar and worshipped the Lord who had saved him. God promised that never again would he destroy the world by a flood. The rainbow in the sky was a sign of God's promise that he would continue to preserve the earth and its people.

BIBLE SEARCH
READ GENESIS 6:5,13–22; 7:11–24; 8:13–22.
Find out:
Why God sent the flood
How Noah built the ark
What happened when the flood came
What took place after the flood.

HERE AGAIN ARE THE HEADLINES

- By disobeying God, human beings brought sin, suffering, and death into the world.

- God still loved the people he had created, even though they had sinned and deserved nothing but punishment.

- God's promise to his fallen creatures gave them hope. He would still carry out his great plan by rescuing them from sin.

KEY BIBLE PASSAGE GENESIS 3:8,9

When Adam and Eve sinned, they ruined their happy relationship with God. Sin was now like a barrier between them and God.

Why did Adam and Eve hide from God?

Why did God come looking for Adam and Eve? How does this show that he still cared about them?

FOR US TODAY

The fall of Adam and Eve into sin explains why there is evil, suffering, and death in our world. This helps us to understand why people do not naturally love God or want to serve him, why they are selfish and find it hard to love one another. It explains why **we** are sinners, and why things go wrong in our lives. It shows us why we must die.

* Read Genesis 6:5 and Psalm 51:5.
  Why do we find it much easier to do wrong than to do right?

Although we are sinful people in a wicked world, God still loves us.

* Read Genesis 8:20-22 and 9:1-17.
  What does God's promise mean for us?
  Why does God still let us live from day to day, even though we do not deserve this?
  How does God make a new start with us every day?

FAMILY TIME

Read the story of Cain and Abel in Genesis 4:1–15. Talk with your family about how sin spoils family relationships, and of the joy which comes through God's forgiveness.

MORE TO DO

1. Find examples of news headlines which show how sinful human beings are. Find further examples which show how God helps and saves people.

2. Prepare a newspaper article (with pictures) telling the story of Noah building the ark.

3. Read Genesis 9:1–17. Why could we call this story 'The New Creation'?

4. Read Genesis 11:1–9. Why did the people want to build a big tower? How did God punish the people?

5. If a time-line is being prepared in your class, begin to fill it out with the main people and events of this chapter.

WORSHIP

A CONFESSION OF SINS:
Almighty God, our Maker and Redeemer, we confess to you that by nature we are sinful and unclean, and that we have sinned against you by thought, word and deed. Therefore we flee for refuge to your infinite mercy, seeking and imploring your grace, for the sake of our Lord Jesus Christ. Amen.

Scripture references: Genesis chapters 3 to 9.

Chosen by God

If your teacher at school told you to pick a team for a sports competition, how would you decide whom to choose in your team?

God chose certain people to carry out his plan. How do you think God decided which people he would choose?

A CHOSEN NATION

Noah's descendants were not faithful to God. They were more interested in making a name for themselves than in honouring God. God punished their pride by making them speak different languages and scattering them into new lands.

But God's plan was to save people from their sin and to bring them back to himself. He decided to have one nation as his special people through whom he would carry out his plan.

Which nation would God choose? Was there any nation good enough to be God's special people?

God decided to **create** a nation. He selected one man to be the father of the nation which would be God's holy people.

GOD CALLS ABRAHAM

The man God chose was called Abraham, who lived in the city of Ur in Babylonia.

One day God said to Abraham: 'Move away to another country which I will show you. I will make you into a great nation. Through you my blessing will come to all nations.'

What a promise that was! But how could Abraham be sure God would keep his word? How could he know exactly what God was planning?

It must have been hard for Abraham to obey this command. But, because he trusted God's word, he moved to the land of Canaan. God said to him: 'This is the land I will give to your descendants'. Abraham built an altar there and worshipped the Lord.

BIBLE SEARCH

READ GENESIS 12:1–7.

How would you have felt if you were Abraham, and God told you to move to a strange land?

Why did Abraham obey God?

READ GENESIS 17:1–8.

What promises did God make to Abraham?

Why did God repeat these promises?

A TEST OF FAITH

It was even harder for Abraham to believe God's promise that he would be the father of a great nation. He and his wife, Sarah, were already quite old, and had no children. Abraham thought he could make the promise come true by having a son from Sarah's maid, Hagar. But God told him this was not the child through whom he would make a great nation.

One night God told Abraham in a vision to count the stars. 'That's how many descendants you will have', he said. He made a covenant, or solemn agreement, with Abraham: 'I will be your God and the God of your descendants'. He told Abraham to circumcise all the males in his household as a reminder of this covenant.

Some time later, three messengers from God visited Abraham. They told him that within a year Sarah would have a son. Sarah could not help laughing. 'That's impossible', she thought. 'I'm already 90. It's too late for me to have a child.' The messengers simply replied: 'Is anything too hard for the Lord?'

The next year, after all the waiting and hoping, God's promise came true. Sarah gave birth to a son, who was named Isaac.

BIBLE SEARCH
READ GENESIS 21:1-6.
Why did God make Abraham and Sarah wait so long to have a son?
Why were Abraham and Sarah so happy when Isaac was born?

THE HARDEST TEST

How precious Isaac, the long-awaited gift of God, must have been to Abraham and Sarah!

Imagine, then, what Abraham must have felt when one day God commanded him: 'Take your son, your only son, Isaac, whom you love, and go to the land of Moriah and offer him there as a burnt offering'!

Why would God command such a thing? He had promised to make a great nation from Abraham. He had given Abraham this son when it was humanly impossible for Sarah to have children. Now Abraham had to kill his son.

Could there be any greater test of Abraham's trust in God?

BIBLE SEARCH
READ GENESIS 22:1-9.
Why was God's command a very hard test for Abraham?
Why did Abraham obey God, even though it was hard for him?

Abraham obeyed God's command. He took Isaac to Mt Moriah, and built an altar there. He tied Isaac up and laid him on the altar. He raised his knife.

Suddenly, the angel of God called to him: 'Do not lay your hand on the lad, or do anything to him; for now I know that you fear God, seeing you have not withheld your son, your only son, from me'.

ONCE MORE THE PROMISE

God was to be trusted. Because Abraham was grateful to God for sparing his son, he offered up a ram as a sacrifice instead of his son.

Again, God gave Abraham his promise: 'I will bless you. Your descendants will be as many as the stars in the sky or the sands on the shore. Through them I will bless all nations.'

THE MAIN POINTS

By calling Abraham, God took an important step in carrying out his great plan.

● God chose Abraham by grace (undeserved love). Abraham was an ordinary sinful person, but God called him and set him apart to be the father of God's holy people.

● God gave Abraham great promises and made a covenant with him:
a great nation would come from Abraham
Abraham's descendants would be given the land of Canaan
all nations would be blessed through Abraham and his descendants.

● Abraham trusted God. He is called 'the father of all believers'.

KEY BIBLE PASSAGE   GENESIS 15:5,6

No one can ever be good enough to deserve God's love. God accepts those people who trust in him.

What does it mean to trust God?

Give examples from the story of how Abraham trusted God.

TIME FOR DISCUSSION

1. Tim Smith said to his pastor: 'God might choose people like you, but he would never choose me. I'm not good enough.' What would you say to Tim?

2. Today God still chooses and calls people to belong to his family. God called you through your baptism.
   Read Galatians 3:26–29.
   How do we become God's children (v 26,27)?
   Who are 'Abraham's descendants' (v 29)?

3. Why can we always trust God, even when it might be hard for us to do this?

WORSHIP

Dear Father in heaven, we do not deserve to be your children. We thank and praise you that you have chosen us by grace to belong to your family. Help us to trust your promises and to do what you want, so that we can show all people what a great God and Father you are. In Jesus' name we pray. Amen.

FAMILY TIME

Talk about what it must be like for a family to have to move to live in another place.

Read Hebrews 11:8–12. Talk about how we can learn from Abraham's great example of faith in God.

SOME EXTRA WORK

1. Trace Abraham's journeys on a map of the Bible world. These texts will help you: Genesis 11:31; 12:5; 12:6; 12:8; 12:10; 13:1–3; 20:1.

2. Read some of the stories of other events in Abraham's life:
   Abraham and Lot: Genesis 13:5–13
   Abraham and Ishmael: Genesis 21:8–21
   Abraham prays for Sodom: Genesis 18:16–33.
   Choose one of these stories and present a brief report to the class at the next lesson.

3. Read Genesis 12:10–20. How does this story show that Abraham's trust in God was not perfect?

4. Find your Baptism Certificate. What was the date and place when God said to you: 'I will be your Father and you will be my child'?

I AM YOUR GOD —

YOU ARE MY PEOPLE!

Scripture references: Genesis 11; 12:1–9; 15; 16:1–4; 18; 21:1–8; 22:1–19.

The Children of Israel

5

Some time ago, a famous film star died leaving a large fortune; but none of his money went to his children. Bitter and angry, they began a court case to try to get their father's money.

Who usually receives the inheritance?
Why do people sometimes squabble over a will?
How may this cause trouble among family members?

God promised to bless Abraham's descendants, to make them a great nation, and to give them the land of Canaan. This blessing would be passed down from one generation to the next. But which son would receive the blessing? This resulted in jealousy and disunity in the family of Isaac and his children. They were weak and sinful people, who often failed God and treated others badly. Yet God kept his promises, even though they did not deserve it. Because of God's blessings, the descendants of Abraham began to grow into a great nation — just as God had planned.

ISAAC AND HIS CHILDREN

Whom would Isaac marry? Abraham wanted his son to marry someone who believed in the true God. So, he arranged for Isaac to marry Rebekah, the daughter of his relative in Mesopotamia, who worshipped the true God.

Isaac and Rebekah waited 20 years for a family. Then God gave them twin sons: Esau and Jacob. Esau was born first, but God had told Rebekah that the younger son would rule over the older. As the boys grew up, the question: Who would receive the promises God had made to Abraham? caused trouble between the two brothers and between their parents. Isaac wanted to give the blessing to Esau because he was born first and was his favourite. But Rebekah wanted Jacob to have the blessing, as God had promised.

When the time came to hand on the blessing, Isaac was old and blind. Rebekah worked out a way for Jacob to trick his father. She told him to pretend to be Esau and to lie to Isaac. In this way Jacob (and not Esau) received the blessing. What God had told Rebekah was coming true.

Esau was furious when he found out what his brother had done. 'The miserable cheat! I'll kill him once Father has died', he threatened. So Jacob had to flee for his life. But where could he go? 'You'll be safe with your uncle in Mesopotamia. Go to him', his mother told him. So Jacob prepared to leave home.

Isaac called Jacob to speak with him before he left. 'Marry one of our relatives in Mesopotamia who worships the true God', he told him. 'May God bless you as he blessed Abraham, and give you possession of this land. God give you many descendants so that you become a great nation.'

Soon after setting out on his journey, Jacob had a strange dream. He saw a stairway reaching to heaven, and heard God speaking to him. God blessed him, giving him the same promises he had made to Abraham. Jacob worshipped God there at the place he called Bethel.

GOD BLESSES JACOB

In the years that followed, God's promise of blessing came true for Jacob. He worked for his uncle Laban and married two of his daughters. He had 12 sons. (From these sons the 'Twelve Tribes of Israel' have descended.)

After many years, Jacob decided to return home to Canaan. As he drew near his home, he grew frightened. Esau was coming to meet him! Did Esau still hate him? Would he try to kill him?

The night before their meeting, as Jacob was praying alone, he had a strange experience. A mysterious visitor came and wrestled with him. (This was really God in human form.) Jacob kept wrestling with him throughout the night. 'I will not let you go unless you bless me', he said. As day dawned, God did bless him. He gave Jacob a new name: Israel, which means 'he struggles with God'. From that day on, Jacob's descendants were called 'the children of Israel' or 'Israelites'.

All was well when Jacob met Esau. The bitterness had gone from Esau's heart. He had forgiven Jacob, and greeted him like a friend. The two brothers lived in peace in different parts of the country.

BIBLE SEARCH
READ GENESIS 28:10–16.
Why did God give Jacob his dream at this time?
What did God promise Jacob?
Why did Jacob call that place Bethel?

 ## GOD SAVES HIS PEOPLE THROUGH JOSEPH

Jacob's favourite son was Joseph. Jacob showed his special love for him by giving him an expensive coat to wear.

Joseph had strange dreams in which his father, mother, and brothers all bowed down to him. All this made Joseph's brothers very jealous and full of hatred. Perhaps they thought that their father intended to give Joseph the inheritance, even though he was not the eldest.

One day they seized him and sold him to be a slave in Egypt. But God looked after Joseph in Egypt. He had great plans for him. Through an amazing chain of events, Pharaoh, king of Egypt, made Joseph governor of the country. God used Joseph to save Egypt from a terrible drought which gripped the whole area. During seven good years, Joseph stored up grain for the seven bad years which followed.

BIBLE SEARCH
READ GENESIS 32:22–30.
Why did Jacob keep wrestling with God?
What amazed Jacob about this experience?
How many people 'wrestle' with God today?

In this way, God also provided for Jacob's family. Since there was no food in Canaan, Joseph arranged for his father and family to come down to Egypt. They settled in the part of Egypt called Goshen. So God used Joseph to save his chosen people.

As Jacob lay dying, he blessed his children. To his son Judah, he gave the special promise that kings and rulers would come from his descendants. Through his tribe, all nations of the earth would be blessed.

The Israelites lived in Egypt for hundreds of years. They grew to be a large nation. God was keeping his promise to Abraham.

BIBLE SEARCH

READ GENESIS 45:5-8.

How did God make evil work out for good? What part did Joseph play in God's plans for his people?

READ GENESIS 46:1-4.

What did God promise Jacob as he left Canaan?

HERE ARE THE MAIN POINTS

- God carried on his plans through people who were weak and sinful. Despite their sinfulness, he kept his promises and passed on his blessing from one generation to the next.

- God cared for the twelve tribes of Israel and blessed them with many descendants, so that they grew to be a large nation.

- God's plan to bless the world centred on this nation. His promise was sure: Through them the Saviour would come.

KEY BIBLE PASSAGE GENESIS 32:9-12

God looked after his people and protected them in danger because of his grace. Those who trusted God realized that they were not worthy of God's blessing.

Why was Jacob unworthy?
Why did God bless him? How did he work through Jacob?
How did Jacob show his faith in God?

Give other examples in these stories of how God blessed people and worked through them, even though they were not worthy.

GOD'S PEOPLE TODAY

1. We are God's people today only because of his grace. Discuss what this means. Read Ephesians 2:8–10.
> Why don't we deserve God's blessing?
> Why can we be sure of forgiveness?

2. Talk about how we may sometimes be like Esau, Jacob, or Joseph's brothers.
How can God work through us, despite our sinfulness?
Discuss how we can show that we are God's people.

WORSHIP

A RESPONSIVE PRAYER:

Dear God, long ago you gave many promises to the fathers of the Israelites;
> **Thank you for giving us your Word and making us your children.**

In wonderful ways you protected the Israelites and made them a large nation;
> **We praise you for letting us be part of your great Christian family.**

You led the fathers of the Israelites to trust in you and blessed them;
> **Help us to grow in faith and to show our love for you.**
> **Grant us your blessing, for Jesus' sake.** Amen.

FAMILY TIME

Talk about special blessings which your family has received, and make a list of them.
Prepare a thank-you prayer, referring to some of these blessings.

Use Ephesians 1:3–6 for a family devotion. Use your thank-you prayer, and close with the hymn: 'Now thank we all our God'.

MORE CHALLENGES

1. If you are preparing a time-line of Bible history, fill in the names of Abraham, Isaac, Jacob, Joseph.

2. A common theme of the stories in this lesson is how people cheat each other. Find out how people deceived others in these stories:
Genesis 29:15–28; 31:17–21; 37:30–32.
Talk about how we may be tempted to cheat others today.

3. See if you can discover the names of the 'Twelve Tribes of Israel'. Numbers 1:20–42 will help you.

4. Interview elderly persons in the congregation (perhaps your own grandparents), and ask them about blessings they have received from God. Report to the class what they said.

5. Members of the class could choose one of the following, read it, and then report to the class on the story:
Esau and the birthright: Genesis 25:29–34
Joseph's dreams: Genesis 37:3–11
Pharaoh's dream: Genesis 41:14–41
Joseph's death: Genesis 50:22–26.

Scripture references: Genesis 24; 25:19–34; 27–33; 37; 39–50.

6

'Set my people free!'

Can you imagine what it would be like to be a slave? In the old days, a slave belonged to his master.
He had no rights; his master could do whatever he liked with him.
How would you feel if you were somebody's slave?
If you were a slave, what would be the best news you could ever have?

A NATION OF SLAVES

Many years after Joseph died, things started to go badly for the Israelites in Egypt. The Pharaohs (rulers) made them work as slaves, building the Egyptian cities. One of the Pharaohs commanded that all Israelite baby boys should be killed, because the Egyptians were afraid that the Israelites were becoming too powerful.

Had God forgotten his people and the promise he had made that they would be a great nation in their own land?

GOD SAVES MOSES

God had not given up his great plan. Another important stage in God's master plan began with the birth of a special baby in Egypt.

An Israelite mother saved her baby boy from the Pharaoh's cruel command by putting him in a basket and hiding him among the reeds at the edge of the River Nile. A daughter of Pharaoh found the baby and adopted him. She called the boy Moses, and brought him up as an Egyptian in Pharaoh's palace.

But Moses knew that he belonged to the people of Israel. He was sad to see how cruelly his people were being treated. One day he saw an Egyptian slave-master kill an Israelite. In anger, Moses killed the Egyptian. When Pharaoh heard of this, Moses had to flee for his life.

GOD CALLS MOSES

Moses spent the next forty years as a shepherd in the desert country of Midian.

One day Moses had a strange experience. He saw a bush which was on fire, but was not being burnt up. A voice spoke from the burning bush: 'I am the God of your ancestors, the God of Abraham, Isaac, and Jacob'.

Moses was terrified. What was God going to do with him? The Lord said: 'I know how cruelly my people are being treated in Egypt. I have come down to rescue them from the Egyptians. Now I am sending you to Pharaoh so that you can lead my people out of his country.'

This was too much for Moses. 'I'm nobody', he said. 'How can I go to Pharaoh and bring the Israelites out of Egypt?' He made excuses to try to get out of this mission. But God promised: 'I will be with you, and my great power will work through you'. God also told Moses to take his brother, Aaron, with him to do the speaking before Pharaoh.

BIBLE SEARCH
READ EXODUS 2:23–25 and 3:1–15.

Why did God want the Israelites to be rescued from Egypt?

Talk about God's name which he made known to Moses.

'LET MY PEOPLE GO!'

Moses and Aaron went to face Pharaoh with God's message: 'The Lord, the God of Israel, says: "Let my people go so that they can serve me!"' But Pharaoh was not impressed. 'Who is the Lord?' he asked. 'Why should I listen to him and let Israel go?'

Now God began to use his mighty power to force Pharaoh to let the Israelites go. He sent one plague after the other on the Egyptians, until the land was almost ruined. Sometimes when a plague struck, Pharaoh promised to let the people go. But whenever God stopped the plague, Pharaoh stubbornly changed his mind.

GOD SAVES HIS PEOPLE

Finally, God told Moses he would send just one more plague which would force Pharaoh to let them go. The Israelites were commanded to get ready to leave Egypt. God told them to kill a lamb and paint the blood of the lamb on the doorposts of their houses.

That night, the angel of death went throughout the land, killing the eldest son in every family — except in those homes that had the blood of the lamb painted on them. The angel passed over those homes.

A terrible wailing filled the land. In the middle of the night, Pharaoh called Moses and said: 'Get out! You and your Israelites! Leave my country! Go and worship the Lord, as you asked!'

At once the Israelites set out from Egypt on the journey that would bring them to the land of their fathers. God led the huge crowd by a pillar of cloud during the day and by a pillar of fire at night.

This was surely a night to remember — the night of their rescue from slavery in Egypt! God commanded the people to celebrate the 'Passover' festival every year to remind them how he had saved them when the angel of death 'passed over' their houses.

BIBLE SEARCH
READ EXODUS 12:1–4.

Why did God want the Israelites to celebrate the Passover?

Instead of the Israelite children dying, the Passover lamb died. Talk about this.

ANOTHER GREAT RESCUE

When Pharaoh realized that his slaves had escaped from his clutches, he chased after them with his army. The Israelites began to panic when they saw they were trapped at the shores of the Red Sea, with the Egyptians coming up behind them.

'Don't be afraid', Moses told them. 'The Lord will fight for you, and there is no need for you to do anything.' Moses held out his hand over the sea, and God parted the waters, so that the people could cross on dry land. The Egyptians followed them. But at God's command, Moses again held out his hand over the sea, and the waters came together. Pharaoh's army was drowned. The Israelites were safe.

God's great power had rescued his people. The Israelites celebrated with songs praising God, their rescuer. God had remembered his covenant, and was carrying out his plan. He saved his people so that through them he could bless all people.

BIBLE SEARCH
READ EXODUS 15:1-13.
What had the Israelites learnt about God?
Find words from Israel's victory song which are true for us, in our lives.

ACCORDING TO PLAN

- God remembered his people and his promises to their ancestors.

- By his almighty power God rescued his people from slavery. Through Moses he led them out of Egypt so that they could serve him.

- God's people celebrated their rescue. This was the beginning of their history as a separate nation.

KEY BIBLE PASSAGE   EXODUS 6:2-8

The people of Israel could do nothing to save themselves. Only the almighty God could set them free.

Find all the statements of God in this passage that begin with 'I will . . .'
What do these promises of God teach us about him?

FOR US TODAY

1. In some ways, our story is like the story of the Israelites in Egypt.
Read Romans 6:17,18.

     In what ways are we slaves? Why can we not set ourselves free from this slavery?

     What reason do we have for giving thanks to God? How can we show that we are thankful that God has set us free?

2. Whenever the people of Israel celebrated the Passover, it was just as if they were re-living the story of their rescue (the Exodus) all over again.

     Talk about ways in which we today celebrate the great things God has done to rescue us. (For example, at Christmas and Easter.)

WORSHIP

RESPONSIVE PRAYER:

I will sing to the Lord :
  Because he has won a glorious victory.
The Lord is my strong defender :
  He is the one who has saved me.
He is my God :
  And I will praise him.
My father's God :
  And I will sing about his greatness.

Scripture reference: Exodus 1–15.

WITH YOUR FAMILY

Talk with your family about times when God has set them free from trouble, sickness, worry, fear.
Read Psalm 105:1–4, and discuss the meaning for your family.

SOMETHING EXTRA

1. Find out what were the ten plagues which came on Egypt. They are listed in Exodus 7:17 – 11:6. Make a chart picturing the plagues. Display the chart.

2. Read the story of Moses' birth and the early years of his life in Exodus 2:1–15. Use the stories in this lesson to begin making a comic book of the life of Moses. Complete it after the next lesson.

3. Perhaps you would like to act out one of the stories about Moses. You could prepare a short play and use it in class. Or you could act out a Passover celebration.

4. Find out about the building of the Egyptian pyramids. This may give you an idea of what life was like for the Israelites under the rule of the Pharaohs.

A people set apart

In July 1982, Prince William was born in London — second in line to the British throne.
From the moment of his birth he was set apart as a special person, someone who might one day be king.

What would it be like to be a member of the royal family? How would you be different from other people? Why would life often be difficult?

God freed the Israelites from the Egyptians so that they could be a separate, holy nation.
They were to be a people set apart, different from all other nations.
Now God intended to make his covenant with them, and
to show them what it meant to be his special people.

THE SINAI DIARIES

'Free at last!' That was how the Israelites felt after God had saved them from Pharaoh. But now they faced a hard journey as God led them across the desert to Mt Sinai.

Suppose you were one of the Israelites and kept a diary of what happened on this journey. Here are some extracts of what you might have written . . .

April 20: It's so hot in the desert. I always seem to be thirsty. My feet are sore from so much walking. Mum is getting worried that we won't have enough food.
The people are good at complaining! I heard some of them grumbling to Moses today about what a bad time we're having. One even suggested that we were better off in Egypt. He sure isn't very thankful!

May 15: God is really looking after us! We arrived at this bad place in the desert. The people were growling that they had no food. Then God promised to give us meat for tea and bread for breakfast. We wondered how ever this could happen.
Then, just as it was getting dark, thousands of birds flew past and settled near the camp. Dad said they were quails, and went out with us to catch as many as we could. Mum cooked them for tea. It was great to have fresh meat for a change.

May 16: This morning God did give us bread for breakfast! When we got up, we saw all this white, flaky-looking stuff lying around the camp. 'Whatever is it?' everyone asked. We tasted it, and it was good to eat. We called it **manna**. God has promised to give us this food every morning.

June 2: More complaining! This time we were out of water. But once again God did something wonderful for us. Moses stood in front of a solid-looking rock. He struck it with his stick — and guess what? Water came flowing out! We all had a long, cool drink. Was I glad!

June 14: At last we have arrived at this big, rocky mountain in the desert called Sinai. God made a special agreement with us today through Moses:

'I am the God who brought you safely out of Egypt. I have looked after you day by day. You are my special people. I have set you apart from all other nations. You are like kings and priests for me. Now you must obey my commandments and keep my covenant.'

June 15: The men built a fence all around the bottom of the mountain today to set it apart as a holy place. Moses warned us that anyone who went on the mountain would die. God is going to appear on the mountain in three days' time! I'm scared to think that God will appear. I wonder what he will be like?

June 18: It's hard to write this. I'm still so scared! Loud cracks of thunder woke us up this morning. We all rushed outside. The whole mountain-top was covered with thick smoke shooting up into the sky. Lightning flashed through the smoke. Suddenly the ground began to shake as though there were an earthquake. Everyone was scared stiff.

Then a trumpet started sounding from the mountain. It kept on getting louder and louder. Suddenly a voice like thunder boomed down from the mountain:

'I am the Lord your God . . . You shall have no other gods before me.'

God gave us his Ten Commandments. He told us what he expected of us as his people. But his voice was so loud and frightening that the people couldn't stand it. They begged Moses to speak for God.

June 19: Today God made his covenant with us through Moses. Moses read all God's commandments to the people and offered up sacrifices.

'We will do everything the Lord has said', the people cried out. Then Moses sprinkled blood over the altar and over us, and said: 'With this blood God seals his agreement with us'. I hope the people stick to it! God told Moses to come up to him. I saw him climbing up, and then he disappeared in the smoke. Boy! he must have been frightened!

BIBLE SEARCH

What were the Ten Commandments God gave the Israelites at Sinai?

READ EXODUS 20:1–17.

32

July 26: It's nearly forty days since Moses went up the mountain. I wonder what he's doing? The people are saying that he won't come back. They told Aaron to make a god which they could see — like the gods in Egypt. So Aaron has made a golden calf and set it up for the people to worship. It all seems wrong to me!

July 28: The people seem to have gone mad. There's been a wild party for days around the golden calf. A lot of the people have got drunk. I reckon God must be terribly angry. He told us not to worship idols!

July 29: It's been a terrible day! You can hear wailing all through the camp. Many people have died. Earlier today, Moses came down from the mountain with two tablets of stone. He saw what the people were doing and was so angry that he broke the tablets on the ground. 'How dare you worship idols!' he shouted. 'Don't you know you belong to God?' Then he sent the Levites through the camp to punish the people. Thousands were killed.

BIBLE SEARCH

Read about the special tent (called the tabernacle) which Moses and the people built

EXODUS 35:4–19; 40:34–38.

August 23: I'm glad that terrible time is past! Although God was very angry with us, he will still have us as his people. It's amazing how much God loves us and puts up with us. But we must obey God's commandments! Moses has come down from the mountain again. He says that God wants us to build a special tent-church as his holy place. A pillar of cloud will rest over it. This will be the sign that God is with us. I want to give some of my pocket-money to help with the building. It will be good to have a place where we can worship God.

GETTING THE MAIN POINTS

- God set the Israelites apart as his special people. Through them he planned to bless the world.

- God made his covenant with the whole nation: 'I am your God. You are my people. You shall be holy as I am holy.'

- God gave the Commandments to keep the Israelites as his holy nation, and to show them how to live as his people.

- God cared for his people in the desert, and taught them to trust him as their God.

- God was very patient with them. He forgave them when they sinned and turned to him for mercy.

KEY BIBLE PASSAGE   DEUTERONOMY 7:6–11

God chose the Israelites to be his own people because of his grace, and to keep the promises he had made to their forefathers.

What could the Israelites expect of God?
What did he expect of them?
Why did God call them a 'kingdom of priests' (Exodus 19:6)?

Keep its promises
destroy enemies

Set apart for a special task

Keep its commandments
Trust to love for him

33

FOR GOD'S PEOPLE TODAY

1. Jim had moved to a new school. Some of his class made fun of him when they found out that he attended church. 'Why do I have to be different from the other kids and go to church?' he asked his mother when he got home. What might his mother have said?
   Read 1 Peter 2:9–10.
   How does Peter describe the people of God?
   How can we serve God as his holy people?

2. 'The Ten Commandments are out of date. No one takes them seriously nowadays.'
   How would you answer if someone said this to you?
   Why has God given us the Commandments?

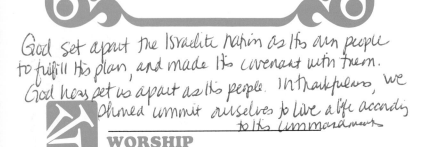

what we do & say is part of our testimony to declare God's wonderful deeds + show we have been called out of darkness I nd want. we know that to visit to [illegible] Lo.

God set apart the Israelite Nation as its own people to fulfill His plan, and made Its covenant with them. God has set us apart as Its people. In thankfulness, we should commit ourselves to live a life according to Its commandments

WORSHIP

Dear Lord, you have called us to be your holy people; you have set us apart as those who belong to you. Help us to show, by what we say and how we live, that we do belong to you. Through Jesus Christ our Lord. Amen.

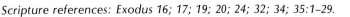

Scripture references: Exodus 16; 17; 19; 20; 24; 32; 34; 35:1–29.

FAMILY EXTRA

Quiz your family to see if they remember the Ten Commandments.

As a devotion, read Deuteronomy 6:4–9 and talk about how you as a family can keep before you the Ten Commandments.

MORE TO DO

1. Other wonderful things happened to the Israelites in the desert. Read about some of them:
   How bitter water was made sweet: Exodus 15:22–25
   How God appeared to the elders of Israel: Exodus 24:9–11, and to Moses: Exodus 33:18–23
   How Moses went up to God on the mountain a second time: Exodus 34:1–9
   How his face shone when he came back to camp: Exodus 34:29–35.

2. During this week, keep a diary. Write down day-by-day problems you have faced, and ways in which God helped you and showed his care for you.

3. Read about the special altar, called the ark of the covenant, which stood in the holy of holies in the tabernacle: Exodus 25:10–22.

4. As a class, decide on some good rules for living as a Christian. Write them on a poster and display them in class.

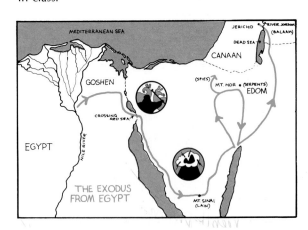

THE EXODUS FROM EGYPT

The land of promise

8

Look at these headlines. Each is quite different, yet each deals with the same problem: the need of people to have land in which to live.

Why are people so concerned to have a land of their own?

What are refugees? What is life like for them?

REFUGEES FLEE FROM SAVAGE FIGHTING

LAND RIGHTS FOR ABORIGIN

BORDER FIGHTING BREAKS OUT!

After leaving Egypt, the Israelites were refugees for many years. They had no land of their own, and had to wander around in the desert. Life was often not easy for them.

But God's plan was to keep his promise to Abraham, and to give his chosen people a land where they could live as a separate nation.

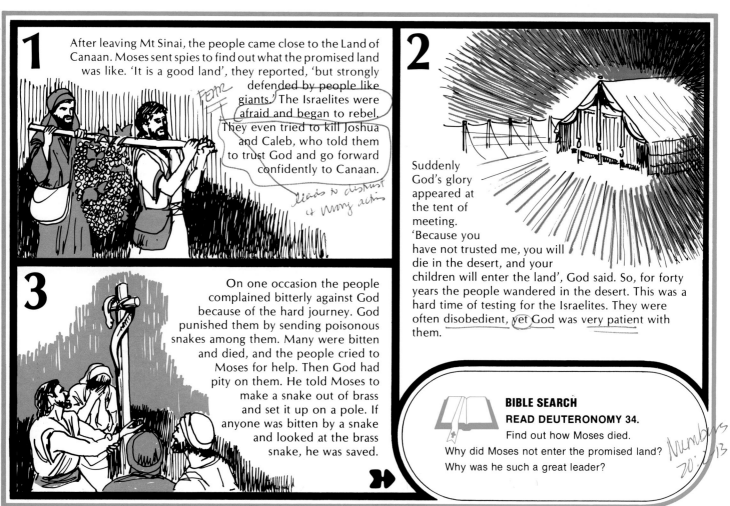

1 After leaving Mt Sinai, the people came close to the Land of Canaan. Moses sent spies to find out what the promised land was like. 'It is a good land', they reported, 'but strongly defended by people like giants.' The Israelites were afraid and began to rebel. They even tried to kill Joshua and Caleb, who told them to trust God and go forward confidently to Canaan.

2 Suddenly God's glory appeared at the tent of meeting. 'Because you have not trusted me, you will die in the desert, and your children will enter the land', God said. So, for forty years the people wandered in the desert. This was a hard time of testing for the Israelites. They were often disobedient, yet God was very patient with them.

3 On one occasion the people complained bitterly against God because of the hard journey. God punished them by sending poisonous snakes among them. Many were bitten and died, and the people cried to Moses for help. Then God had pity on them. He told Moses to make a snake out of brass and set it up on a pole. If anyone was bitten by a snake and looked at the brass snake, he was saved.

BIBLE SEARCH
READ DEUTERONOMY 34.
Find out how Moses died.
Why did Moses not enter the promised land?
Why was he such a great leader?

35

4

After forty years in the desert, the Israelites marched into the country east of the River Jordan. There they won great victories. So Balak, king of Moab, called on Balaam, a famous prophet, to curse the Israelites in God's name. But when he tried to curse them, he could only bless them and say: 'There shall come a star out of Jacob. He shall be king and ruler.'

5

Moses died before the Israelites entered Canaan, and Joshua became the new leader. He led the people to the border of Canaan, near Jericho. With God's help, he set out to conquer the land. First, they had to cross the River Jordan. God worked a miracle: as the priests carried the ark in front of the army to the river, the water stopped flowing, and they could cross on dry land. At last the Israelites were in the promised land.

6

The first city to be conquered was Jericho. At the Lord's command, the Israelites marched around the city walls once each day for six days with the ark in front, and with seven priests blowing horns. On the seventh day, they marched around seven times, ending with a great blast from the horns and loud shouting. Suddenly, with a loud crash, the walls of Jericho fell down. God had given the city into their hands; and, at his command, they completely destroyed it.

7

As the Israelites set about conquering the whole land, God was with them, giving them other wonderful victories. In the south, the Israelites put five princes to flight, and a great hail-storm sent by God killed many as they fled. When the northern princes combined their armies to fight Joshua, the Israelites had another great victory, capturing and destroying Hazor, the capital city of the Canaanites.

BIBLE SEARCH

The heathen tribes of Canaan were destroyed by the Israelites. This was God's punishment of those wicked people, and part of his plan that the Israelites should live as a separate people in a land of their own. This was necessary to carry out God's plans to bless the whole world through them.

READ NUMBERS 21:1–3.

What vow did the Israelites make?

How did God answer their prayer?

READ DEUTERONOMY 18:9–12.

Why did God let the Israelites drive out the Canaanites?

8 After years of fighting, Canaan finally belonged to the Israelites. God had given them the land he had promised.

Yet they did not fully obey God. They let Canaanites live on in parts of the land, and great trouble came on them later because of this.

Before he died, Joshua reminded the twelve tribes once more of God's goodness, and urged them to be faithful to him. He set up a memorial stone as a reminder of God's covenant.

BIBLE SEARCH

Find out how Joshua made the people promise to serve the true God and remember his covenant.

READ JOSHUA 24:1,2, 14–18.

What was Joshua's final reminder and warning (verses 19,20)?

How did he try to keep them faithful (verses 25–27)?

THIS STORY TEACHES US

- God gave the Israelites the land of Canaan so that they could live as a separate nation. He promised to keep them as his holy people and, according to his plan, to bless the world through them.

- The Israelites did not get the land by means of their own strength. God gave it to them. He expected them to serve him as their God, and to show thanks to him as they cared for the land he had given.

- God reminded his people again and again of who they were. He warned them of the danger of becoming like the heathen tribes around them, and told them never to forget that they belonged to him.

KEY BIBLE PASSAGE   DEUTERONOMY 26:1–11, 18, 19

The Israelites were continually to remember their history which showed how God had made them his people and had blessed them.

Find verses which tell how the Israelites —
 remembered who they were
 remembered to whom they belonged
 showed they were thankful
 remembered God's plans for them.

'The promised land was God's gift, not just won by the Israelites through their own strength.' Discuss.

GOD'S PEOPLE TODAY

1. God has given **us** a land filled with good things.
Read Acts 14:17.
>What are some of the good things we enjoy because of the land God has given us?
>Why does God bless us with these gifts?

2. 'God has given us the land and all its resources to use and to look after.'
Discuss.
>How can we be good caretakers of our country and of the good things God gives us?
>How can we show that we are thankful?

 WORSHIP

Dear heavenly Father:
You blessed the Israelites by giving them a land of their own;
you have shown us your love by giving us our country and the many good things we need for daily life.
Help us to live as your people, and to use for your glory the gifts you have given us.
In Jesus' name we pray. Amen.

Scripture references: Numbers 13; 14:1–28; 21:4–9, 21–25; 22; 24:14–19; Joshua 1; 2–4; 6; 10; 11; 24.

 TIME WITH THE FAMILY

If your class discovered facts about our country (see below, point 5, **Something Extra**), share this information with your family. Ask them what things in nature especially appeal to them.

As a devotion: Members of the family list things for which the family is thankful. Then read Psalm 136:1–3, and thank God for the things you have listed, in the same way that the psalm does.

SOMETHING EXTRA

1. What else are we told about the Israelites' journey in the desert? Read some more interesting stories about —
>rebellion against Moses (Numbers 16:1–5, 28–34)
>Moses' disobedience (Numbers 20:2–13)
>the spies in Jericho (Joshua 2).

2. Each day Israelite families confessed their faith in God. Read what they said (Deuteronomy 6:4,5).

3. Why does obeying God bring blessing? Why does trouble follow disobedience? Read what God told the Israelites about this (Deuteronomy 28:1–20).

4. Find a map which shows how the land was divided among the twelve tribes of Israel.

5. As a class project, find out some facts about our country; for example, its size, population, and agricultural and industrial products.

9

Judges to the rescue

'Following the leader' is not just a game children play. We all follow leaders — and this has a great influence on our lives. Bad leaders can get us into trouble. Good leaders can keep us out of trouble, or even rescue us when we get into trouble.
Give examples of how leaders can hurt or help us.
Why is it so important to follow the right kind of leaders?

How would the people of Israel behave in their new home? Would they live as God's holy people? This was what God wanted. He had given them the land of Canaan as part of his plan to keep them a separate nation.

As long as Joshua lived, the people were faithful to God. Joshua was a good, strong leader who helped the Israelites to be true to their Lord. But when Joshua and his generation died, the Israelites forgot the Lord who had rescued them from Egypt. They began to follow the example of their heathen neighbours by worshipping idols (false gods).

LED INTO IDOLATRY

God had told the Israelites to drive the heathen tribes out of Canaan and to destroy all their altars. But they did not obey God's command fully. Some Canaanites remained in the land, and often led the Israelites into idolatry.

The Canaanites had a religion of magic and superstition. Their legends taught that El was the father of the gods, and Asherah was the mother. They had a family of 70 gods and goddesses, the most important god being Baal, the lord of nature.

The Canaanites offered sacrifices to their idols, believing that this would make sure that they had good crops and prosperity.

Again and again the Israelites became unfaithful to God, and began worshipping Baals. To punish them, God let raiders attack and defeat them. These raiders would plunder their land, and cause the Israelites great hardship. But when the people called on God to help them in their trouble, God sent them good, strong leaders to rescue them. These leaders were not kings, but were called judges.

The Book of Judges tells this story — of how the Israelites were unfaithful to God, and of how God remained faithful to them, and sent judges to the rescue. It is a story which goes in a cycle.

A STORY WHICH GOES IN A CYCLE

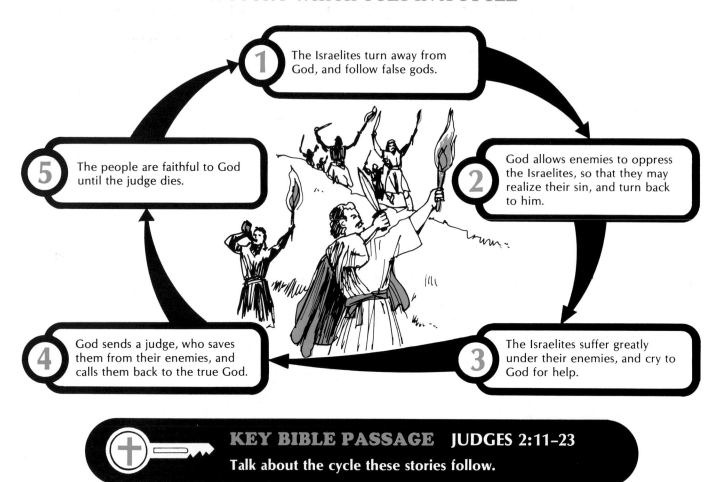

1 The Israelites turn away from God, and follow false gods.

2 God allows enemies to oppress the Israelites, so that they may realize their sin, and turn back to him.

3 The Israelites suffer greatly under their enemies, and cry to God for help.

4 God sends a judge, who saves them from their enemies, and calls them back to the true God.

5 The people are faithful to God until the judge dies.

KEY BIBLE PASSAGE   JUDGES 2:11–23

Talk about the cycle these stories follow.

This cycle is seen in the story of Gideon, one of the most important judges.

GIDEON SAVES HIS PEOPLE

Once again the Israelites had turned away from God. They were in danger of ceasing to be God's special people, and of becoming heathen like the nations round about. So God sent the Midianites to punish them. These people were a wandering tribe from the desert, who raided the Israelites, and plundered their land.

God chose a young farmer called Gideon to rescue the Israelites from these invaders. The Spirit of God came on him and filled him with courage to lead his people against their enemies. As a sign that God was with him, Gideon broke down the idols of Baal and Asherah in his home town. When the Midianites came up with a huge army to plunder the land of Israel, he summoned Israelites from all the tribes round about to fight against them.

32,000 Israelites gathered under Gideon. But God said the army was too big. He would give him the victory with just a few men. So, Gideon sent most of them home again. With only 300 men, he attacked the Midianite camp in the dead of night. Holding burning torches hidden in jars, his band of men surrounded the sleeping Midianites. Suddenly, they smashed the jars and shouted loudly.

BIBLE SEARCH

Find out more about Gideon:

the signs God gave him
(JUDGES 6:36–40)

how he chose his soldiers
(JUDGES 7:2–8)

the victory God gave him
(JUDGES 7:16–25).

Hearing the noise, the Midianites were terrified and fled in panic. The Israelite soldiers came from everywhere, chasing them out of their country and destroying their army. God had given his people a great victory. Now they could live in peace.

Through Gideon, God led the Israelites to turn away from idols and to be faithful to him and his covenant. As long as Gideon lived, the people followed the God of Abraham, Isaac, and Jacob.

SAMUEL: THE PROPHET SENT BY GOD

Hannah, the wife of Elkanah, was sad because she had no child. One day she came to Shiloh where the priests had set up the house of the Lord. 'If you give me a baby boy', she prayed to God, 'I will dedicate him to your service.' God heard her prayer, and some time later Samuel was born.

Hannah kept her promise. When Samuel was about three years old, Hannah brought him to live with the High Priest, Eli, in Shiloh. Samuel grew up in the house of the Lord.

God was with Samuel in a special way. He became judge after Eli, and was a prophet of the Lord, speaking God's Word to the people. He travelled throughout the country, teaching the Israelites, calling on them to be faithful, and leading them in the worship of the true God. He encouraged them in their fight against their enemies, called the Philistines.

Samuel was an important man in God's plans. He united the people in the worship of the true God, and prepared the way for the coming of the first king.

BIBLE SEARCH

God was with Samuel in a special way. Read how God first spoke to him **(1 SAMUEL 3:1-15).**

How was Samuel different from other judges?

Why was he an important person in God's plans?

THESE ARE THE MAIN POINTS

- ● God did not give up his people when they turned away from him and began to serve false gods, like the heathen tribes round them.

- ● God led the Israelites to realize their sinfulness by allowing trouble to come on them. He sent strong leaders to lead them back to him, and to rescue them from their enemies.

- ● Through these leaders, God helped the Israelites to remain a special people through whom he would bless the world.

How was God working out His plan: Promises God made + to whom:

pg. 16   pg. 21   pg. 25   pg. 45

Gen 3:15   point #2   top   point #3 → MESSIAH (JESUS)

ADAM   ABRAHAM   JUDAH   DAVID

FOR US TODAY

The life of the Israelites went in a cycle; our lives often follow a similar pattern. Think about this story:

> Bob had a bad temper. Sometimes he lost control of himself and started fighting. This often got him into trouble. His friends would tell him to cool down. Later Bob felt badly about what he had done. He would ask God to forgive him and to help him overcome his bad temper. What cycle was Bob's life following?

Read 1 John 1:5–10.
> Give examples of how we are unfaithful to God in our daily life. How does God lead us back to him?

FAMILY EXTRA

Talk about how people have helped your family in time of trouble. (Share an example of such help at the next class session.)

MORE ACTIVITIES

1. Read about the adventures of some other judges:
Deborah and Barak (Judges 4:1–16)
Jephthah (Judges 11:29–39)
Ehud (Judges 3:12–30).

2. Fill in your time-line. Dates for this period are not certain; these are what some scholars propose: Moses, c. 1300; Joshua, c. 1250; time of Judges, 1200–1050.

3. Read the exciting story of Samson, the strong man (Judges 13–16). Talk about how Samson was strong, yet very weak.

4. Make a poster, **GOD WORKS THROUGH PEOPLE**, using pictures of some of the stories in the book of Judges.

WORSHIP

CONFESSION AND ABSOLUTION:

All: Lord God, we confess that we have sinned against you in thought, word, and deed. Forgive us, and help us to be faithful to you. Amen.

Leader: God has forgiven our sins for Jesus' sake. May he comfort us by his forgiveness, and strengthen us to live as his people. In Jesus' name. Amen.

GOD WORKS THROUGH PEOPLE

Scripture references: Judges 2:11–23; 6–8; 13–16; 1 Samuel 1; 3; 7.

A king for God's people

George Washington . . . Winston Churchill . . . Adolf Hitler . . . Joseph Stalin. These men were all important leaders — but were they good or bad for their country?

It makes a difference to a country what kind of leaders it has. Why?

'Give us a king!' the Israelites begged Samuel. 'Why can't we be like the other nations, and have a king to lead us?' 'God is your king', Samuel answered. 'He rules over you, and helps you against your enemies.' He warned them of the danger of having an earthly king.

But the people wanted a leader to unite them as a nation and make them strong. And in the end God gave them kings. The king was to be God's special servant, chosen by him to rule over his people.

With the coming of the kings, God's plans entered a new stage. To one of these kings he gave the special promise that his royal line would never end. Through this family, God would keep his promise to save the world from sin and death.

THE SAD STORY OF SAUL

The first king in Israel was Saul, from the tribe of Benjamin. At a gathering of the people, Samuel poured oil over his head, as a sign that God had made him their king.

At first Saul was a good ruler. He worked hard to unite the people and to save them from their enemies. But as he grew older, Saul became jealous and suspicious. He disobeyed God and forgot that he was God's **servant**, and began to use his power for himself.

Saul had failed God and the people.

CHOSEN TO BE KING

Long before Saul died, God told Samuel to go to Bethlehem, to the family of Jesse of the tribe of Judah. There he was to anoint another man to be king. Jesse's youngest son, a young shepherd-boy, was called David. 'This is the man I have chosen', God told Samuel. 'Anoint him.' So, Samuel took oil, and poured it over David's head as a sign that God had chosen him. But Samuel kept this a secret from Saul.

After many years of trial and hardship, David became king, and united all the tribes of Israel under his rule. Under his strong rule, the Israelites defeated their enemies. He captured the city of Jerusalem, and made it his capital. The kingdom of Israel now included all the country which God had promised Abraham.

43

Suppose that David wrote his memoirs in his old age.
Here are some of the things he might have written as he thought back over his life:

FROM THE KING'S MEMOIRS

I've come a long way in my life — all the way from shepherd-boy to king! As I look back, I can see how God led and blessed me every step of the way.

God chose me to be king when I was only a lad looking after my father's sheep in Bethlehem. I don't know why God chose me. I could only trust him to be with me and to keep his promise.

I know he was with me when I went out to fight the Philistine giant, Goliath. The Lord gave me victory that day. And then, when Saul became jealous of my popularity and tried to kill me, God looked after me. He went with me when I had to flee for my life out into the desert and live in the wild with a band of outlaws.

God gave me a friend — what a friend! Prince Jonathan, Saul's son — dearer to me than a brother. O Jonathan, Jonathan, how I miss you! My heart still aches when I remember the day you and King Saul died in battle. Yet God works in strange ways. With Saul dead, the people of Judah came and made me king. God kept his promise to me. At the age of 30, I became king over all Israel.

God has been with me in my rule as king. I give him the credit for the many great victories over our enemies. The Lord also helped me to make our people a strong nation. More than anything, I wanted to unite the people in worshipping God by building a temple here in Jerusalem. It was a great disappointment when the prophet Nathan gave me God's message that I would not be allowed to build the temple. My son would be given this honour.

But I soon forgot my disappointment when God gave me a wonderful promise: 'The line of kings from your family will never end'. I wonder just what he meant. Would a son of David always be king? One thing I'm sure of: in some way God will use my family in his plans to bless all people.

God's grace amazes me. When I think of how greatly I sinned by committing adultery with Bathsheba and having her husband killed, I know that I deserved God's punishment. Looking back, I can see how great trouble has come on my family and the whole nation because of what I did. But God forgave me, and did not take the kingdom away from me. Surely, goodness and mercy have followed me all the days of my life!

Soon I will die. As I look back over my life, I can only sing the praises of the Lord, who has been my Shepherd. He will be with me even when I walk through the valley of the shadow of death. I am not afraid. I know I am safe in his keeping.

BIBLE SEARCH

Read some more stories from the life of King David:

how he faced Goliath **(1 SAMUEL 17:4–11, 31–52)**
his friendship with Jonathan **(1 SAMUEL 20:17–42)**
how he sinned with Bathsheba **(2 SAMUEL 11)**
how he sang to the Lord as 'the Sweet Psalmist of Israel' **(2 SAMUEL 23:1–5)**.

THE TEMPLE IS BUILT

After David died, Solomon became king. He was the son of David and Bathsheba. God chose him to build the temple. Under his leadership, the people worked for seven years to complete the beautiful house of God. After it was dedicated, the priests and Levites led the Israelites in daily worship of God in the temple.

Solomon ruled over a large and united kingdom, in which the Israelites lived in peace and prosperity. God blessed Solomon so that he became famous for his wisdom and great wealth.

But this king, too, failed God and his people. He married many heathen women, and even built temples for their idols. He taxed the people heavily until they began to grumble. In this way, Solomon sowed the seeds of division among the twelve tribes. He was the last king to rule over a united Israel.

BIBLE SEARCH

Read about Solomon's wisdom and his prosperous reign
(1 KINGS 3:16–28; 4:20–25).

Why did Israel become a great nation in Solomon's reign?

Why did his reign lead to future trouble and division?

ACCORDING TO PLAN

- God gave the Israelites kings as his anointed servants to unite them and to keep them safe as his people.

- God blessed his people through these kings, even though they were sinful people. The worship of God at the temple in Jerusalem united the people as a nation set apart for God.

- God was working out his plan to bless the whole world. He promised David that a special king would come from his family, who would rule for ever.

KEY BIBLE PASSAGE   2 SAMUEL 7:25–29

The promise made to David was an important step forward in God's plan to save the world.

Talk about the way God's plan is gradually unfolding.

ADAM	ABRAHAM	JUDAH	DAVID	MESSIAH
Gen 3:15	pg. 21 pt #2	pg. 25 top	pg. 45 #3	

FAMILY TIME

Make up a quiz about the life of King David, and see how many of the questions your family can get right.

As a devotion, read Psalm 23 and talk about what it means that God is our Good Shepherd. As a prayer, you could read the hymn: 'The King of love my shepherd is'.

MORE CHALLENGES

1. Fill in the names of the first three kings of Israel on your time-line (Saul, c. 1030–1010; David, c. 1010–970; Solomon, c. 970–930).

2. Read more about these three kings of Israel:
Saul (1 Samuel 15:10–22)
David (1 Samuel 23:19–24)
Solomon (1 Kings 3:4–14).

3. Give examples from this story of ways in which:
the kings failed God and the people;

God used them for good despite their sinfulness.

4. On a cassette, record an imaginary interview with David after he killed Goliath, and the Israelites defeated the Philistines.

GOD'S PEOPLE TODAY

 1. God is our King, yet we also live under earthly rulers. God places these rulers over us as his servants to work for him.

Read Romans 13:1–5.
Why does God give us rulers?
How should God's people regard the government?
Talk about our duties to our country.

2. What difference is there between the rule of the kings of Israel and our modern governments?

WORSHIP

Dear heavenly Father, we thank you for giving us earthly rulers who preserve peace and good order in our country. Help us to honour and respect those you have placed over us, and to live as your people. Through Jesus Christ our Lord. Amen.

1 Peter 2:13–17

Scripture references: 1 Samuel 8; 10:17–23; 14:47–52; 15; 16–31; 2 Samuel 1; 2; 5; 7; 11; 12; 15–18; 1 Kings 1; 3; 6–9; 11.

God's people worship

11

Bob says that he believes in God, but he never goes to church, reads the Bible, or prays to God.

Is it possible to believe in God, and not worship him?

What does it really mean to worship God?

Why do we build churches in which to worship God?

What an exciting day it was for the people of Israel when Solomon's temple was dedicated! This magnificent building was God's house. Here God would come to them to speak to them through his servants, to bless and forgive them. They would gather to hear God's Word, to praise God, to offer sacrifices to him. The temple was their worship centre.

Worship was always important in the story of God's people, right from the beginning. In worship God said again and again to Israel: 'You are my people and I will bless you'. And the people responded: 'You are our God, and we will serve you'.

So the worship of the Israelites played an important part in God's plan to keep them as his holy people. God gave them special instructions so that their worship would be different from that of the heathen nations around them. And in these worship instructions there were many hints of how God would carry out his plan to bless all people.

In this chapter, we look at some details of Israel's worship in the Old Testament.

WORSHIP PLACES

- **ALTARS** In the early days, the people had no special buildings for worship. They built altars of earth or stones.

- **TABERNACLE** In the desert, God commanded the Israelites to make a tabernacle (tent of meeting) as a special place of worship. The tabernacle had two rooms: the holy place, and the holy of holies where the ark of the covenant was kept. The Israelites took the tabernacle with them into the promised land.

- **TEMPLE** Later, Solomon built a beautiful temple, modelled on the tabernacle. This became Israel's worship centre.

WORSHIP LEADERS

- **PRIESTS** God appointed Aaron and his male descendants as priests to lead the worship. Priests offered sacrifices, and taught the people God's commandments.

- **HIGH PRIEST** He was the 'go-between' for God and the people. He spoke for God, and gave the people God's blessing. Once a year the high priest entered the holy of holies with a special sacrifice for the sins of the Israelites.

BIBLE SEARCH
READ PSALM 100.

The worship of Israel grew out of their special relationship with God.

What was the relationship between God and his people?
How did this relationship make a difference to the people's worship?

SACRIFICES (worship acts)

In their worship the people offered gifts, or sacrifices, to God.

- **SIN-OFFERINGS** — Animals (especially lambs) were killed and offered to God for the sins of the people. By these sacrifices, the people said to God: 'We are sorry for our sins. Have mercy on us.' God accepted their offering, and forgave them.

- **THANK-OFFERINGS** — The people gave grain and vegetables to God, and said: 'Thank you for blessing us'.

WORSHIP TIMES

Special times were set aside to worship God.

- **EVERY DAY** — Priests offered morning and evening sacrifices.

- **SABBATH** — Saturday was a day of rest. The people came together for worship.

- **FESTIVALS** — There were many holy days on which Israel worshipped God. For example:

   The Passover (March)
   Pentecost (May) and **Tabernacles** (October) were harvest festivals
   Day of Atonement (September-October); the high priest appeared before God in the holy of holies with special sacrifices for the sins of all the people.

WORSHIP SONGS

The people of Israel wrote many hymns and songs to use in their worship. There are 150 of these in the book of Psalms. There are different kinds of psalms:
   praise and thanksgiving (such as Psalm 136)
   prayers for help and protection (Psalm 28)
   prayers for mercy and forgiveness (Psalm 51)
   confession of faith in God (Psalm 104)
   prayers asking God to punish enemies of God and of the people (Psalm 83).

Some psalms are personal, telling of one person's feelings (Psalm 5). Other songs are for the nation or for the king (Psalm 72). Choirs often led the singing of psalms, and the people would respond.

BIBLE SEARCH

READ PSALM 23.

Why did King David trust God?

Talk about some of the things David trusted God to do.

Who is our Good Shepherd?

A LIFE OF WORSHIP

God wanted Israel to worship him with their whole life. Everything they did was to please God and honour him. In several books of the Old Testament, God taught his people how to live a life of worship. He guided them as they faced life's problems, and told them how to act and think wisely.

These books of wisdom and guidance are: Job, Proverbs, Ecclesiastes (The Preacher), and the Song of Solomon.

GETTING THE POINT

Worship was an important means God used to carry out his plan to keep Israel as a holy nation.

● In worship, God came to the people to speak his Word — to warn, guide, forgive, bless, and strengthen them.

● In worship, God's people responded to him with thanks and praise, and turned to him for help in time of need.

● Through the directions God gave his people for their worship, he pointed forward to the coming of the Saviour, who would be the perfect High Priest.

KEY BIBLE PASSAGE   PSALM 95:1–7

God-fearing Israelites were glad to come together to praise God. Through worship they were helped to live as his people.

Who is the God whom the Israelites worshipped?

Why were they glad to worship him?

How did they worship God?

GOD'S PEOPLE NOW

1. The life of God's people today also centres on worship. Discuss how God blesses and strengthens us through worship.

   Read Ephesians 5:19,20.
      What advice does the apostle give?
      Why does our worship always centre on Christ?

2. God gives us pastors to lead in worship.
      In which ways is a pastor like a priest?
      Why can we say that every Christian is a priest of God?

3. We worship God in our homes. We also build churches where we can come together for worship.
      Why do we try to make our churches beautiful buildings?
      Talk about some of the furnishings in your church. How are they used in worship?

WORSHIP

Scripture references: Genesis 12:8; Exodus 25–27; 30; 1 Kings 6; 8; Leviticus 1–4; 8; 23.

SUGGESTIONS FOR THE FAMILY

Ask members of your family whether they have a favourite hymn or Bible verse. Ask them why it is special to them. Make a list of their choices. You could use these for your devotions as a family.

For a family devotion, read Psalm 95:1–7. Let each person mention something for which to thank God. Close by saying: 'We give thanks to the Lord, for he is good, and his steadfast love endures for ever. Amen.'

EXTRA ACTIVITIES

1. Find out more about the worship of the Israelites:
      the holy place (read Hebrews 9:1–10)
      the festivals (read Leviticus 23)
      the sacrifices (read Leviticus 1:2–9; 2:1–3).
Talk about what the worship of Israel pointed forward to.

2. Draw a plan of the tabernacle or of Solomon's temple, and explain the different parts of the plan.

3. Look up the following psalms, and decide when each one would help you most:
Psalms 32; 103; 121; 8.

Draw a poster to illustrate Psalm 23. Learn the psalm.

4. Find as many pictures as you can of Christian churches, and display them in the classroom. Discuss how they are the same and how they are different (both on the outside and in the inside).

5. How did Jesus our Lord use the book of Psalms? Compare Psalm 118:22,23 with Matthew 21:42; Psalm 22:1 with Matthew 27:46; Psalm 31:5 with Luke 23:46.

12

A faithful remnant

Could the Christian church survive in Red China? It seemed impossible. For many years, public worship was forbidden, and many Christians were persecuted. But as soon as people could again worship publicly, it was discovered that there were now *more Christians in China than ever before.*

During all those years, faithful Christians kept on worshipping and witnessing, and through them God kept his Church alive.

Talk about this remarkable story. How did God work through a small group of faithful believers?

A small group of faithful believers in Israel, called a remnant, was important in God's plan to save the world. After King Solomon, more and more of the Israelites turned away from God to worship idols, and became like their heathen neighbours. Yet God always preserved a few people who remained true to the covenant he had made with their fathers. Through this remnant of believers, God kept alive his plan that a Saviour would come through the nation he had chosen.

NEWS OF THE DAY

What happened during the time of the kings of Israel after Solomon? If there had been newspapers in those days, you might have read articles like those below.

ABOUT 930 BC

Jerusalem Journal

Jerusalem

NORTHERNERS REBEL!

The ten northern tribes have revolted. At a fiery meeting yesterday at Shechem, King Rehoboam, Solomon's son, rejected northern demands for lower taxes and fairer treatment. In response to the king's tough line, the northerners, under the leadership of Jeroboam, have said they will break with the south and elect their own king. In Jerusalem, Rehoboam has now put the armies of Judah and Benjamin on full alert. Civil war is likely. Tension and rumour are running high in the capital. People are asking whether a divided Israel can survive against our enemies.

Reign of King Ahab   Northern Kingdom

ABOUT 870 BC

SAMARITAN TIMES

MASSACRE OF PROPHETS!

Hundreds of the Lord's prophets were slaughtered today by command of King Ahab and Queen Jezebel. Prophets of Baal and Asherah have been installed in the capital. Their gods are now to be worshipped throughout the land. 'We want a prosperous kingdom', Jezebel said today. 'We'll worship gods which bring good luck and good times.'

BIBLE SEARCH

Read how King Rehoboam caused the kingdom to be divided **(1 KINGS 12:1–17).**

How did this weaken the nation?

SAMARITAN TIMES

MT CARMEL

AMAZING SCENE AT CARMEL

A dramatic meeting took place here today between the prophet Elijah and leaders of the people. 'Make up your minds', Elijah told them. 'If the Lord is God, worship him. If Baal is god, worship him. Let's put our gods to the test. We'll each build altars here on the mountain and call on our god to send down fire to burn up our offerings. Then we'll see who is the true God.'

Elijah and the people stood watching as the prophets cried to Baal around their altar. Silence! Nothing happened! At last Elijah prayed to the Lord God. With a great blast of heat and flame, fire fell from heaven and burnt Elijah's sacrifice, scorching the ground all around.

People were terrified and threw themselves on the ground in fear. 'The Lord is God', they cried. They had made their choice! At Elijah's command, they seized the prophets of Baal and put them all to death.

SAMARITAN TIMES

Report from our correspondent at Mt Sinai

Strange things happened here today! Elijah fled here to save his life because Jezebel has vowed to kill him. He seemed to be in despair at first. 'I am the only one left who worships you', he complained to God. 'What has happened to all your great plans for us?'

God answered in a frightening way. An earthquake shook the mountain, followed by a great storm of fire and wind. Then Elijah heard a soft whispering voice which sent shivers down his spine. It was God speaking: 'There are still 7000 people in Israel who worship me, and have not bowed the knee to Baal'.

Elijah has left Sinai now. He seems to have fresh hope. 'God is still in charge', he reported. 'He still has people through whom he can carry out his plans.'

BIBLE SEARCH
Read how God took Elijah to heaven **(2 KINGS 2:9–13).**

Why did Elisha ask for special power to do God's work?

SAMARITAN TIMES

SURVIVAL THREATENED

Assyria in the north and Egypt in the south are steadily increasing their pressure on Israel, according to the minister for foreign affairs. 'The Assyrians now directly threaten us', he told cabinet today. 'The position is desperate; our survival is at stake.'

The prophet Hosea later confirmed these fears. 'Listen to God's warnings', he told people in the market-place. 'Turn back to him before it is too late, and ask him to forgive you. We are completely dependent on God in the face of this enemy.'

BIBLE SEARCH
Read how King Hezekiah led the people in Judah back to God **(2 KINGS 18:1–8).**

Discover how God helped Hezekiah in time of great trouble **(2 KINGS 19:8–19,35,36).**

52

ABOUT 722 BC

Jerusalem Journal

KINGDOM OF ISRAEL DESTROYED

The northern kingdom is destroyed. Assyria now controls all of Samaria. Invading forces under King Shalmaneser have captured the capital. Thousands have been slaughtered, and survivors are being sent into exile in Assyria. This is a tragic day for our nation!

'This is God's doing', the prophet Isaiah commented today. 'He has punished his faithless people. Let us take warning and repent, or else God's punishment will strike Judah!'

● JERUSALEM

ABOUT 620 BC

Jerusalem Journal

RADICAL CLEAN-UP BY JOSIAH

King Josiah has begun a thorough reform in Judah. Idols are being burnt, their altars torn down, and priests sacked. 'We will keep the covenant of the God of our fathers', the king proclaimed.

'Reform your hearts also', prophet Jeremiah warned today. 'Don't trust in the temple and boast that no harm can come to you. God will surely send Babylon to punish us if we do not turn to him in true faith.'

Only a few in Judah did remain faithful. By about 500 BC, Judah, too, was 'ripe for judgment', and its survival was threatened.

HERE AGAIN ARE THE HEADLINES

● God warned his people that he would punish them when they turned away from him to worship false gods. The threat from powerful nations surrounding Israel showed God's people how completely they depended on him.

● When the northern tribes refused to listen, God allowed the Assyrians to destroy their kingdom and wipe them out as a separate people.

● God kept a remnant of people true to him during this whole period. Through the people who loved and served him, God carried on his plans to save the world through the descendants of Abraham.

KEY BIBLE PASSAGE   1 KINGS 19:9–18

God was working in strange, quiet ways to keep people faithful to him, even though Elijah did not realize this.

Why did Elijah feel so discouraged?

How did God encourage him?

Why were the few people still faithful to God so important for his plans?

GOD'S PEOPLE TODAY

1. Many people are unfaithful to God today. How does God keep some people faithful to him?
Why are these people like a remnant in the world?

Read Matthew 5:13–16.
How can we be like salt?
How can we let our light shine?

2. 'It's OK — everyone's doing it!' people sometimes say after they have done something wrong.

Why shouldn't God's people just follow what 'most people' do?

What is to be their guide?

WORSHIP

Heavenly Father, keep us faithful to you, even though many turn away and no longer serve you. Help us to set a godly example. Fill us with hope, even in time of trouble, because we know you are in charge. In Jesus' name we pray. Amen.

Scripture references: 1 Kings 12; 16:29–34; 18; 19; 2 Kings 17; 22; 23; Isaiah 10:1–12; Jeremiah 7:1–7.

FAMILY TIME

Ask your family to help make this mobile about letting your light shine.

For a devotion, read Matthew 5:13–16. Talk about ways in which your family can let its light shine. You could sing the hymn 'This little light of mine', or 'Jesus bids us shine'.

HERE ARE SOME CHALLENGES

1. If you are preparing a time-line, fill in some of the main events of this period.

2. There are many exciting stories in the books of the Kings. Some of these are: Elijah and Ahab (1 Kings 17–22); Elisha's work (2 Kings 3–7); the fall of Samaria (2 Kings 17); King Josiah's reforms (2 Kings 23:1–14). Read one of these stories and report on it to the class. Tell what message it has for us today.

3. Try to 'let your light shine' in some special ways during this week. Here are some ideas: visit a lonely person, or someone in hospital; invite a friend to church; lead in a family devotion; help a neighbour; speak up for someone at school.

4. If you have an older brother or sister who has been confirmed, find out what is on the confirmation certificate. Share the text with your class.

Prophets speak for God

13

An ambassador had been summoned before the Prime Minister of the country in which he was serving. His government had been accused of serious border violations. Now he had to give his country's answer to these charges. He had a great responsibility. The answer he gave could mean war or peace between the two countries.

How does an ambassador represent his country?
Why does he have a great responsibility?

God chose special men to be his ambassadors, or representatives, in Israel. These men were called prophets. They were spokesmen for God. He gave them his Word, and sent them to the people as his special messengers.

God had spoken to Israel through Moses, the greatest prophet in the Old Testament. In the centuries which followed, he sent many more prophets as his servants, to preach his Word and to call on his people to be faithful.

GOD WAS AT WORK THROUGH THE PROPHETS

● **God gave the prophets his Holy Spirit**
The Spirit of God came on these men to give them special power. They could know and declare the will of God. Sometimes they had strange visions.

● **God gave them wisdom**
The prophets could understand what God was saying through the events and happenings of the times. They explained this to the people.

● **God spoke his powerful Word through the prophets**

God warned the people of his punishment
Listen to God speaking through Amos:

'The people of Judah have sinned again and again, and for this I will certainly punish them. They have despised my teachings and have not kept my commands. They have been led astray by the same false gods that their ancestors served!'
(Amos 2:4)

God called on his people to repent
Listen to God speaking through Jeremiah:

'Unfaithful Israel, come back to me . . . You belong to me . . . I am merciful and will not be angry . . . Only admit that you are guilty and that you have rebelled against the LORD, your God.'
(Jeremiah 3:12–14)

God promised to forgive
Listen to God speaking through Isaiah:

'Now, let's settle the matter. You are stained red with sin, but I will wash you as clean as snow. Although your stains are deep red, you will be as white as wool.'
(Isaiah 1:18)

God assured the people of his love
Listen to God speaking through Hosea:

'I will bring my people back to me. I will love them with all my heart; no longer am I angry with them. I will be to the people of Israel like rain in a dry land.'
(Hosea 14:4,5)

God gave his people hope for the future

The prophets pointed to the coming Saviour-King.
(These sayings are called Messianic prophecies.)
Listen to God speaking through Isaiah:

'Just as new branches sprout from a stump, so a new king will arise from among David's descendants. The spirit of the LORD will give him wisdom, and the knowledge and skill to rule his people.'

(Isaiah 11:1,2)

'My devoted servant, with whom I am pleased, will bear the punishment of many and for his sake I will forgive them. And so I will give him a place of honour.'

(Isaiah 53:11,12a)

WHO WERE THE PROPHETS?

- Some prophets did not write down the Word that God gave them, but simply spoke his message to the people.
  Find out who some of these prophets were: 2 Samuel 12:1–7; 2 Kings 3:9–12; 1 Kings 11:28–33. *Nathan Elisha Ahijah*

- Some prophets wrote down the Word that God spoke through them. Their writings are part of the Old Testament.
  Which are the prophetical books of the Old Testament?
  Find their names in the index of your Bible.

- Sometimes false prophets also worked among God's people and misled them. God warned his people against these prophets and their lying messages.
  Read what God says about false prophets: Jeremiah 23:31,32.

PAGES FROM THE PROPHETS' 'WHO's WHO'

Suppose that someone had written a 'Who's Who' of the prophets. Here are some of the more important entries he might have included.

AMOS:
'The man who cried out for justice'.

A shepherd from Tekoa in Judah. Worked in the Northern Kingdom about 770 BC. Faced times of prosperity, but great wickedness.

CENTRAL MESSAGE:
Repent, you wicked people! You oppress the poor; your religion is make-believe; you follow false gods. God will destroy your nation.

FAMOUS SAYING:
'Let justice flow like a stream, and righteousness like a river that never goes dry.'
(Amos 5:24)

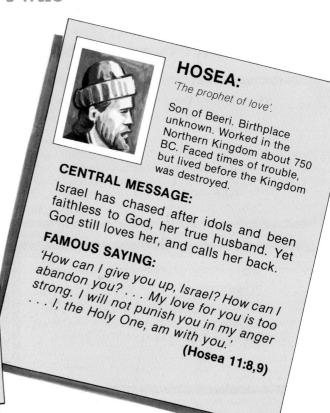

HOSEA:
'The prophet of love'.

Son of Beeri. Birthplace unknown. Worked in the Northern Kingdom about 750 BC. Faced times of trouble, but lived before the Kingdom was destroyed.

CENTRAL MESSAGE:
Israel has chased after idols and been faithless to God, her true husband. Yet God still loves her, and calls her back.

FAMOUS SAYING:
'How can I give you up, Israel? How can I abandon you? . . . My love for you is too strong. I will not punish you in my anger . . . I, the Holy One, am with you.'
(Hosea 11:8,9)

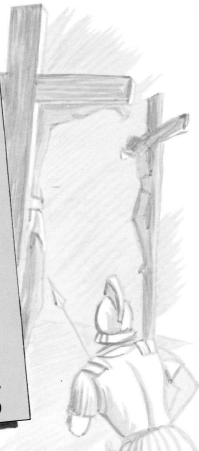

ISAIAH:

'The Gospel preacher of the Old Testament'.

Son of Amoz. Born in Jerusalem. Worked in Jerusalem about 740–710 BC. Lived when Judah's survival was threatened by Assyria.

MANY VITAL MESSAGES — HERE ARE SOME:

God will punish you, faithless Judah. Turn back to God and he will pardon you.

Do not despair in all your troubles. God has not forgotten you. He works all things according to his plans.

God has given you a wonderful hope. There will be a time of world-wide peace when the great king, the Son of David, will come.

God will send his Servant to suffer for us. He will save us from our sins, and gather in God's people from all the nations.

FAMOUS SAYING:

'A child is born to us! A son is given to us! And he will be our ruler. He will be called: "Wonderful Counsellor", "Mighty God", "Eternal Father", "Prince of Peace".'

(Isaiah 9:6,7)

WHAT WE HAVE LEARNT

- The prophets were God's special messengers, who spoke his Word to the people, and called on them to be faithful.

- Most people took no notice of the prophets, but God kept a remnant of believers true to him through the Word of these messengers.

- The prophets spoke first of all for their own time. But God also used them to give clear promises that he would send the Messiah — the Saviour-King.

- The prophets were important in God's plan. Through them, he kept alive the hope that he would bless the world through his chosen people.

KEY BIBLE PASSAGE ISAIAH 55:10–13

God worked through his Word to carry out his plans.

How did God work through the Word spoken by his prophets?

How did God judge those who turned away from him? (Compare Isaiah 10:1–4.)

How did God treat those who turned back to him?

GOD'S PEOPLE TODAY

1. How can we know what God wants? How does he give *us* his Word?

   Read 1 Thessalonians 2:13. *Hebrews 1:1–3*

   How does God speak to his people today?

   How does he use special messengers to give us his Word?

2. One of the announcements in the Sunday Church Bulletin reads: 'A meeting of St Matthew's congregation will be held next Sunday to call a pastor. We encourage all members to attend this important meeting . . .'

   Talk about how pastors are called to serve God's people.

   How do men prepare themselves for this work?

WORSHIP

Thank you, heavenly Father, for speaking to us today and for giving us pastors to proclaim your Word to us. Help us to hear it gladly and to live according to it. For Jesus' sake. Amen.

WITH YOUR FAMILY

Write out the names of the prophets who wrote books in the Old Testament (or find these names in your Bible table of contents). See how many of these prophets are known to your family.

For a family devotion, read what is said about one of the prophets in the 'Who's Who'. Then read 1 Peter 1:10–13, and pray, thanking God for giving us his Word.

MORE THINGS TO DO

1. Here are some important messages God gave through the prophets about his plans for the future. Look up the texts, and discuss what they tell us:

   Isaiah 9:1–3; 53:4,5; Micah 5:2; Jeremiah 23:5,6; Zechariah 9:9; Malachi 3:1.

2. Ask your pastor to show his Call Document to the class. Talk about what is said in this document.

3. Read stories about the prophets in action:
   Elijah and false prophets (1 Kings 22:3–37);
   Elisha and Naaman (2 Kings 5:1–19);
   Isaiah and Hezekiah (2 Kings 20:1–11).

4. Someone in the class could write the story of the prophet Jonah as a short play. You could act it out in class or in some other suitable place.

Scripture references: Deuteronomy 18:14–22; 1 Samuel 10:5–10; Isaiah 6:1–8.

A city destroyed

This is a photo of a city destroyed by bombing and shelling. How does it make you feel? This has happened to hundreds of cities in our time.
Mention some cities destroyed in this way.
Imagine yourself living in one of these cities as it was being destroyed. How would you feel?

In 587 BC, Jerusalem was destroyed and the kingdom of Judah wiped out. The Israelites had sown the seeds of idolatry and wickedness. They reaped a terrible harvest of destruction.

Yet, it was really the goodness of God which allowed this destruction to come on his people. Through their great trouble God wanted to lead his people back to him and make them faithful. He wanted to give them a new beginning and fulfil his promises to bring great blessings on the whole world through his chosen people.

God had been very patient with Israel. Again and again, through his prophets, he had warned that his judgment would come on them. Jeremiah was his special prophet to bring this message to the people in the last days before Jerusalem was destroyed. Sternly, yet lovingly, he warned that God would send a strong enemy who would conquer their land and destroy Jerusalem.

'Turn back to God, before it is too late!' he cried. But the king and his people would not listen. Jeremiah's message made them so angry that they threw him into jail several times.

THE END DRAWS NEAR

A mighty enemy was now threatening the Kingdom of Judah. In 598 BC, King Nebuchadnezzar from Babylon led his armies against Jerusalem. He captured the city and carried away all its treasures. 10,000 people were taken away as slaves, including the king, the princes, and the best of the soldiers and workers. Only the poorest people were allowed to remain.

Even after this, the people who remained were too proud to obey God or listen to Jeremiah. In about 590 BC, Zedekiah, the new king of Judah, rebelled. Nebuchadnezzar came with a great army and laid siege to Jerusalem. The city was doomed!

66 *My eyes are worn out with weeping; my soul is in anguish. I am exhausted with grief at the destruction of my people. Jerusalem lies in ruins. Young and old lie dead in the streets — killed by enemy swords. The Lord has finally done what he threatened to do: He has destroyed us without mercy, as he warned us long ago* 99
(Lamentations 2:11,17,21)

In these words the weeping poet speaks of his deep sorrow and tells how God has finally punished his people.

BIBLE SEARCH
READ JEREMIAH 25:1-14.
Why wouldn't the people listen?
What hope did Jeremiah give for the future?
How does his message show that God is perfectly fair and just?

A LAST CHANCE

Jeremiah sent an urgent message to King Zedekiah. 'God will give the city into the hands of Nebuchadnezzar, who will completely destroy it and burn it to the ground.' When the leaders heard this they wanted to kill Jeremiah, and threw him into a foul, muddy well in the prison. Jeremiah was sure he would die, but he was rescued by a friend and kept in another part of the jail.

King Zedekiah knew that Jerusalem faced a desperate situation. 'What shall I do?' he asked the prophet. Jeremiah urged him to surrender, and warned that otherwise Jerusalem would be completely destroyed. But once again the king would not listen to the prophet's advice.

 ## THE END COMES

For 27 months Jerusalem was besieged. The suffering of the people grew worse and worse. A terrible famine spread through the city and no food was left. Finally, the Babylonians broke through the walls, and the end had come. Zedekiah tried to escape with some of his soldiers, but was captured. Nebuchadnezzar punished the king horribly. Zedekiah had to watch his two sons being killed, and was then blinded. They put him in chains, and took him away as a slave to Babylon.

The Babylonian army captured the whole city, and tore down the walls. The palace, the temple, and all the important houses were burnt. The Israelites suffered greatly. Most of them were carried off as slaves to Babylon. There they lived in exile, sad captives in a strange land.

All seemed hopeless. 'God has punished us for our sins. He has forsaken us', the captives in Babylon cried.

HOPE IN GOD

God **had not** forsaken his people. Through these sad events he was teaching them a lesson which they and their descendants would never forget. Sin had brought terrible punishment, and only God could help them now. They could only trust in him, and cry to him for mercy.

BIBLE SEARCH
READ JEREMIAH 36:4, 20–26.

Why did the king burn the scroll?
Whom was he hurting by doing this?
How did he bring about his own punishment?

> **❝** *Let us examine our ways and turn back to the LORD. We have sinned and rebelled [against the LORD]. My tears will pour out in a ceaseless stream until the LORD looks down from heaven and sees us* **❞**

(Lamentations 3:40,42,49)

Even in exile there was hope for the people. Jeremiah wrote to the captives: 'Build houses; plant gardens. Marry and have children. God has not forgotten you. He will end your captivity. After 70 years he will bring you back to your own land.'

So, there in a foreign land, by the banks of strange rivers, the Israelites sadly waited for God, in his mercy, to give them a new beginning.

This is the hope of the poet:

> **❝** *The Lord's unfailing love and mercy still continue, fresh as the morning, as sure as the sunrise. The Lord is all I have, and so I put my hope in him* **❞**

(Lamentations 3:22–24)

BIBLE SEARCH
READ PSALM 137:1-6.

Why did the Israelites in Babylon long so much for their old land?

How had they learnt to appreciate what they had lost?

THE MAIN POINTS

● God allowed great suffering to come on his people.
His judgment fell on them because they kept on sinning and would not listen. Yet, even this trouble was according to God's plan. In this way he taught them that being his covenant people meant obeying him.

● God used the suffering to draw his people closer to himself.
He led them to be truly sorry for their sin and to cry to him for mercy and help. He showed them how completely dependent they were on him.

● God gave them hope, even in their captivity.
Through his prophets he promised to help them and to restore them to their own land. All was not lost! God still had great plans for them, and for the whole world through them.

KEY BIBLE PASSAGE   2 CHRONICLES 36:13–21

'No one makes a fool of God.'

Why is this a good summary of what the Scripture passage says?

What did God teach his people through the destruction of Jerusalem? How did he want them to respond?

FOR US TODAY

1. 'A person will reap exactly what he sows' (Galatians 6:7). What does this mean? Is it always true? Give examples of how this may happen in a person's life. Why do we never need to despair, even though we may have gone wrong?

2. Why is there suffering and trouble in the world? Read 2 Corinthians 4:17; Hebrews 12:11; 1 Peter 1:6,7.

    How does God use suffering for the good of his people today? Tell how suffering or trouble has been good for you personally.

WORSHIP

Pray these verses:

O thou from whom all goodness flows,
I lift my heart to thee;
In all my sorrows, conflicts, woes,
Dear Lord, remember me.

When on my aching, burdened heart
My sins lie heavily,
Thy pardon grant, new peace impart,
In love remember me.

WITH YOUR FAMILY

Talk to your parents or grandparents about times of hardship or suffering they have experienced. Ask them whether the trouble was good for them.

As a family devotion, read Lamentations 3:22–33 and pray, thanking God for his promise to help us in trouble. You could finish by reading or singing the hymn 'Beloved, it is well'.

MORE TO DO

1. Find out more about the great prophet Jeremiah. Discover:

    why he is called 'the weeping prophet' (Jeremiah 8:18 – 9:11; 15:10–12; 20:1–2; 26:7–15)

    how he gave messages to God's people in strange ways (Jeremiah 13:1–6; 19:1–11; 27:1–7)

    what happened to him when Nebuchadnezzar conquered Jerusalem (Jeremiah 40:1–6).

Discuss why his work was so sad and hard, and yet so important for God.

2. 'The Israelites brought trouble on themselves. They had no one to blame but themselves.' Do you agree/disagree?

3. As a class project, or individually, prepare a map showing Palestine and Babylon. Mark on the map the important places and the Israelites' journey into exile. Compare this with Abraham's journey when God called him.

4. 'The destruction caused by war is God's judgment on sin.' Do you agree/disagree? Can any good come out of war? How will God end all the trouble in the world?

5. Find a story of someone who has suffered greatly, but has found great blessings from God through his suffering.

Scripture references: Jeremiah 1:1–10; 4; 5; 29:1–25; 38; 39; 2 Kings 25.

A new beginning

15

Daniel faced a difficult decision. King Darius of Babylon had made a strict law: 'If anyone prays to God during the next thirty days, he will be thrown into a pit full of lions.'

Daniel had always prayed to God three times a day. What would he do now?

What did Daniel do? How did God look after him? Who was Daniel? Why was his example so important for the Israelite exiles in Babylon?

Talk about the life of these Israelites, and the difficulties they faced.

'I have not forgotten you. Be patient and trust me', God told the Israelites in Babylon. 'After 70 years you will return to your own land.'

This promise of God offered great comfort to the exiles. With the terrible destruction of Jerusalem still fresh in their memories, they turned to God for help. Even though they had no temple, they worshipped God in Babylon. They had come to understand more fully now that God is not bound to one country, but is the Lord of the whole earth.

Many of the exiles prospered in Babylon and gradually came to be contented with their new country. But some of them always had a deep longing to return to Canaan and to rebuild the temple. They wanted to be God's separate people once again, living in a land of their own. So, they waited patiently for God to keep his promise.

HELP AND ENCOURAGEMENT

God sent prophets and leaders to encourage his people in exile. They urged the Israelites to trust in the Lord, and to remain true to him.

For many years the prophet Ezekiel spoke the Word of God to the people, and reminded them that they still belonged to God. 'Trust in God', he told them. 'He will lead you back to the mountains and streams of Israel, just as a shepherd gathers his scattered sheep.'

BIBLE SEARCH
READ EZEKIEL 37:1-4.
Why was the Israelite nation in captivity like a valley full of dry bones?

What hope did God give the exiles?

Why did the Israelites have to depend completely on God?

63

A faithful leader like Daniel helped the Israelites to remember that they were God's people.

God blessed Daniel with great wisdom, so that he became a counsellor of the King of Babylon. God spoke through him to his people about the time when the Messiah would come to establish his kingdom. Daniel's faithfulness in remaining true to God encouraged the Israelites also to follow the God of their fathers.

Among the Israelite leaders were three young men who refused to bow down to an idol which King Nebuchadnezzar commanded all to worship. When the king had them thrown into a furnace of fire, God protected them so that not a hair of their head was hurt. Their brave witness to God helped their people to remain faithful.

GOD CONTROLS HISTORY

At last the time came for Babylon to be punished for its wickedness and cruelty. The Persians, under King Cyrus, destroyed the Babylonian Empire and established a new kingdom. About 70 years after the first Israelites were taken away as captives to Babylon, God led King Cyrus to make a proclamation throughout all his kingdom. It read:

> " *This is the command of Cyrus, Emperor of Persia. The LORD, the God of Heaven, has made me ruler over the whole world ... May God be with all of you who are his people. You are to go to Jerusalem and rebuild the temple of* " *the LORD, the God of Israel*
>
> **(Ezra 1:2,3)**

A NEW BEGINNING

This was good news! God's promise had come true. With joy and thankfulness, about 40,000 Israelites, led by Zerubbabel and Joshua, set out to return to their own land. Once again God was working through a remnant, to make a new beginning. The Israelites did not return empty-handed. They took with them generous gifts from those who stayed behind. King Cyrus gave them back all the precious temple vessels Nebuchadnezzar had taken, so that they could be used once again for God's service.

Imagine the joy of the Israelites when, after a long and tiring journey, they finally saw the hills and valleys of their homeland! After all these years, to be back in Jerusalem, the ruined city they loved so much! They settled in the city and villages round about, thankful that God had brought them home again. Because that part of Canaan was known as Judea, they came to be called Judeans, or Jews.

 BIBLE SEARCH

Read about the return of the Israelites to Palestine:
EZRA 2:1,2,70; 3:1-6.

Why was life hard for the new settlers?
What was one of the first things they did? Why?

THE TEMPLE REBUILT

Things were not easy for the settlers as they began to build new homes in the land God had given their forefathers. But one of the first things they did was to build an altar to the Lord, and to worship God. It took them many years, however, to rebuild the temple. Jealous enemies made their work hard and caused them much trouble. But, encouraged by the prophets Haggai and Zechariah, the Jews finished the work, and dedicated the new temple in a joyful ceremony.

Now the people began once again to celebrate the Passover festival. They praised God for his goodness and the new beginning he had given them.

Many years later, under a leader called Nehemiah, the Israelites also rebuilt the walls of Jerusalem, and the city could prosper.

God had been very good to the Israelites. In his mercy he had re-established them in the land of their fathers. God had kept his promise. They could trust him to protect and bless them.

BIBLE SEARCH
READ HAGGAI 2:1–9.

How did God encourage the people?

Why was completing the temple important for the people?

THESE ARE THE HEADLINES

- God was still with his people in Babylon. He called on them to trust him, and to wait patiently for him to fulfil his promises.

- God was in charge. Empires rose and fell according to his will. Finally he made it possible for his people to return to the land he had given them.

- God gave the Israelites a new beginning. In their homeland they could once again live as his separate people. Gradually he was unfolding his plan to save the world through his chosen people.

KEY BIBLE PASSAGE   ISAIAH 40:1–5; 9–11

Who really led the Israelites back to their own land?
Talk about: how the prophet pictures the return to Canaan
              how the Israelites felt about it.

GOD'S PEOPLE TODAY

1. God has given all his people today a new beginning. Read 2 Corinthians 5:17,18.

    Talk about what this means for us.

2. A pop star tells how he became a drug addict, and in despair thought of committing suicide. Then he was led to Jesus, and found fresh hope in the Gospel. 'God helped me to start life all over again', he told his friends.

    What difficulties would this man experience in his new life?
    How could his friends help him?

3. The Israelites experienced that God is faithful.

    Why can we be sure that God will never forsake us, even in trouble (see 1 Peter 5:10)?

  WORSHIP

RESPONSIVE PRAYER:

For loving us as our faithful God;
For leading us to trust you :
   We praise you, Father.
For making us new people through Christ;
For helping us live the new life day by day :
   We thank you, Father, through Jesus Christ our Lord.

Bible references: Ezekiel 20:33–44; Daniel 6; 9:1–9; Ezra 1; 2; 3; 6:13–22; Nehemiah 2:1–8; 2:17–20; 6:15–16.

 INVOLVE THE FAMILY

How has it happened that your family is living in this country?

Talk about this, and find out how God then gave your family, or your ancestors, a new beginning.

For a devotion, read Psalm 46 and talk about why we can trust God to keep his promises. Close with a prayer of thanks. You could use the hymn 'Now thank we all our God'.

 **SOMETHING EXTRA**

1. Bring your time-line up to date by marking in the events until the time of Nehemiah — destruction of Jerusalem: 587 BC; return: c. 538 BC; Nehemiah: c. 450 BC.

2. Read how Daniel remained faithful to God in the king's palace: Daniel 1:3–21. Discover one of the strange visions God gave Daniel about the coming of the Messiah and his kingdom: Daniel 7:9,10,13,14.

3. Find out how the Israelites celebrated the Passover after their return home: Ezra 6:19–22. How did this help them remember that they were God's people?

4. Discover how Nehemiah had the walls of Jerusalem completed: Nehemiah 4:14–21; 6:15. Talk about why it was important for the walls to be built.

5. As a project, interview a family who are recent immigrants to this country. Ask them how they feel about this new beginning.

Waiting for the sunrise

16

We spend a lot of time in our life waiting. Give examples of this from your own life. How do you feel as you wait — for a birthday, for example, or for a holiday?

Have you ever waited for the sun to rise? Just before dawn an expectant hush falls over the dark land, as it waits for the light to come. It was like that for God's people living again in the land of Canaan after the return from Babylon. Expectantly they waited for God to fulfil his promises:

- for the time of peace and joy promised by the prophets
- for the great Saviour-King to come and establish his wonderful kingdom
- for God to bless the nations through his people, so that these nations, too, would worship the God of Israel.

But in many ways these years of waiting were dark years — full of great hardship and disappointment.

WAITING FOR GOD TO SPEAK

The Israelites waited for God to speak to them through the great Prophet whom Moses had promised.
But for hundreds of years God remained silent.
However, the Jews did have the record of the great things God had done and said to their fathers — in the writings of the prophets. Under the guidance of a priest from Babylon, called Ezra, they began to gather together the books of Moses and the prophets, and the wise sayings and poetry of God's people.
The Old Testament Bible became the great treasure of the Israelites, and united them as God's people.

WAITING FOR THE MESSIAH TO COME

Many Israelites longed for Messiah to come — the king of David's line who would set them free, and rule in glory.
But for hundreds of years the Jews suffered under the power of foreign kings, who often treated them harshly and cruelly.

BIBLE SEARCH
READ EZRA 7:6-10.
Talk about how God used Ezra to help his people.
READ EZRA 9:1-4; 10:1-4.
Some men in Judea began to marry heathen women. Why did Ezra insist on them sending these wives away?

RULERS OF THE ISRAELITES DURING THIS PERIOD

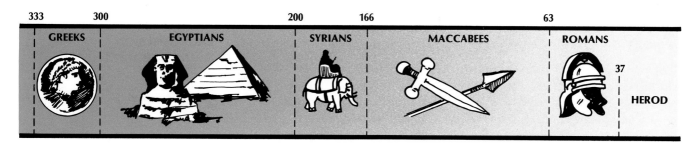

After the Jews had been oppressed for many years by various foreign rulers, a brave family of Jewish priests, called the Maccabees, rebelled and began a guerilla war to set their people free. After much bloodshed, they defeated Antiochus Epiphanes, a wicked Syrian king, and set up their own kingdom.

But there was no real freedom or peace for the common people even then. The Maccabees fought for power among themselves, and were often cruel rulers.

In 63 BC, at a time of great disorder in Palestine, the Romans came and took control. Now the land became part of the Roman Empire, subject to the Emperor.

The Romans made Herod king over Judea in about 36 BC. Herod, too, was a wicked king, and the Jews suffered under his rule.

No wonder the Israelites kept asking: 'When will Messiah come to set us free and bring us peace?'

HOW CAN WE SURVIVE AS WE WAIT?

'God remains silent. Wicked kings oppress us. How can we survive as God's people?' These were anxious questions for many Jews during these difficult years. They answered the problem in various ways:

● Some gave up the special hopes of God's people, and simply adopted the ideas and ways of the people who ruled them. The **Sadducees** in Jesus' time were people like this.

● Some tried to keep the Law of Moses perfectly. Some even drew up long lists of rules to keep. 'If we live as righteous people, God will look after us', they thought. The Law became like God for them. The **Pharisees** in Jesus' time were like this.

● Some **tried to escape from their troubles**. They banded together and went out to live in desert places. Often these people felt sure that the end of the world would come soon, and they planned to be ready.

● Some became **freedom fighters**. They hoped to bring about the new kingdom of peace and freedom by force.

WAITING QUIETLY AND CONFIDENTLY

Yet, through all this time, there was always a **remnant of faithful, God-fearing Jews**. Patiently and quietly they waited for God's kingdom to come — in God's own time, and in his own way. So they trusted in God's mercy, and looked to him for help and blessing.

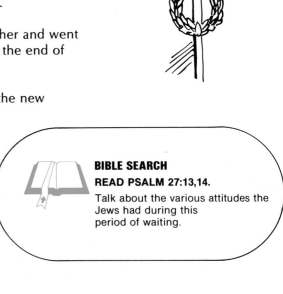

BIBLE SEARCH
READ PSALM 27:13,14.
Talk about the various attitudes the Jews had during this period of waiting.

THE HOPE OF GOD'S PEOPLE

Faithful Jews waited on God, knowing that his promises were sure. Their hopes focused on particular promises which God had made:

THE GREAT SON OF DAVID WILL COME

'I will give them a king like my servant David to be their one shepherd, and he will take care of them. I, the LORD, will be their God, and a king like my servant David will be their ruler. I have spoken.'

(Ezekiel 34:23,24)

The Israelites had great hopes that Messiah would come in God's own glory. But they did not know who Messiah would be or how he would come.

Read Ezekiel 34:20–31.

> *Why could the Israelites wait in hope?*
> *Why was this hard to do?*

GOD WILL MAKE A NEW COVENANT

'The time is coming when I will make a new covenant with the people of Israel . . . I will be their God, and they will be my people . . . I will forgive their sins and I will no longer remember their wrongs.'

(Jeremiah 31:31,33,34)

The old covenant pointed forward to the time when God would bring forgiveness and blessing to the whole world through his people. But the Israelites did not know clearly how God would bring this about.

Read Jeremiah 31:31–34.

> *Why was a new covenant needed?*
> *What would be special about this covenant?*

GOD WILL SEND A SPECIAL MESSENGER

'I will send my messenger to prepare the way for me. Then the Lord you are looking for will suddenly come to his Temple. The messenger you long to see will come and proclaim my covenant.'

(Malachi 3:1)

God told his people to wait for the coming of a prophet with a special work to do.

> *What was his work to be?*

WAITING IN HOPE

From one generation to the other, God's promise to save the world had been handed on:

ADAM → NOAH → ABRAHAM → MOSES → DAVID → PROPHETS → THE REMNANT

And now faithful Israelites waited for the sunrise:

" He will cause the bright dawn of salvation to rise on us and to shine from heaven on all those who live in the dark shadow of death, to guide our steps into the path of peace " **(Luke 1:78,79)**

ACCORDING TO PLAN, THE SAVIOUR WOULD COME

Review the Old Testament stories to see how God's plan to bless the world through his people gradually unfolded.

FOR US TODAY

1. God's people today are also waiting for God to act. They trust him to keep his promises. What are some of these promises?

   Read Luke 11:9–13; 2 Timothy 4:18; 1 John 3:2.

   Talk about them.

2. Old Mrs Jamieson had been bed-ridden for two years. One day, when the pastor encouraged her, she replied, 'I'm asking God to make me patient. I'm sure that in his own good time he will take away my troubles.'

   Talk about Mrs Jamieson's attitude as she waited. How might others have felt in her situation? How does God want us to live as we wait for him to keep his promises?

WORSHIP

Dear God, thank you for giving us such wonderful promises. We know that in your own time and way you will keep all your promises to us. Help us to trust you as we wait. Amen.

WITH YOUR FAMILY

Ask your family to help you make a list of things we wait for as God's people. Write them out, and display them somewhere at home.

For a devotion, read Matthew 5:2–10, and talk about some of the promises Jesus makes to those who love him. Pray, asking God to help us trust his promises.

MORE CHALLENGES

1. We have studied the way God's saving plan developed through the Old Testament. Here are some of the key words we have often heard about: *grace chosen covenant prophecy Messiah remnant.* Explain the meaning of each word. Talk about how they fit into God's plan in the Old Testament.

2. Some important books of the Jews were written during this period, but did not become part of the Hebrew Bible. These books are called the *Apocrypha.* Find out the names and the contents of some of these books.

3. Read the book of Esther to discover how God saved his people when a wicked man tried to destroy the Israelites in Babylon.

4. In Jesus' time many Jews were not living in Palestine, but were scattered about the Roman Empire. How had this happened? Wherever they went, Jews built synagogues and continued to worship the true God. Discuss what a synagogue was, and how worship in the synagogue helped the Israelites to live as God's people.

5. Find Galilee, Samaria, and Judea on a map of Palestine. Jews began to live again in Galilee during the time of the Maccabees. But different people lived in Samaria. Discover who these people were, and how they came to be there (2 Kings 17:24–33).

PART TWO: THE NEW TESTAMENT

The first part of the story of God's saving plan (called the Old Testament) ends with God's people waiting for God to carry out his promise to save them.

The second part of the story (called the New Testament) begins with the exciting news that the time is here. The **one special Person** comes to carry out everything God had planned.

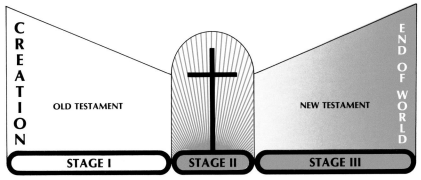

The New Testament proclaims the Good News (Gospel) about this person whom God sends to be the Saviour of the world. It tells the amazing story of **who he is**, and **what he does** according to God's plan. His name is Jesus; he is the Christ (Messiah).

The New Testament tells us how:

- Jesus becomes a human being, lives a perfect life for us, gives up his life to pay for the sins of the world, and wins the victory over sin, death, and the devil;
- Jesus' followers go everywhere telling the Good News that Christ had come to be the Saviour, not just of the Jews, but of **all people**;
- through the work of his apostles, Jesus begins to build his Church — the people of God with whom God makes his new covenant;
- Jesus promises that he will come again to take his people to live with God in perfect happiness for ever — just as God planned in the beginning.

NEW TESTAMENT

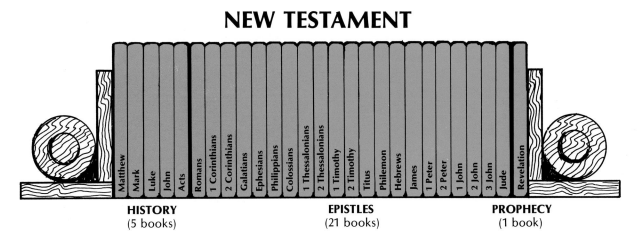

The New Testament was written over a period of about 50 years (45–100 AD) in the Greek language by Evangelists and Apostles. There are three different kinds of writings in the 27 books of the New Testament: books of history, letters (epistles), and a book of prophecy.

NEW TESTAMENT TIME-LINE

The New Testament time-line sets out how God carried out his plan through Jesus, and is unfolding it still today.

Main events and people are pictured by symbols, which are also included in the lesson material. Check where each lesson symbol belongs on the time-line so that you can pinpoint its place in the history of God's plan.

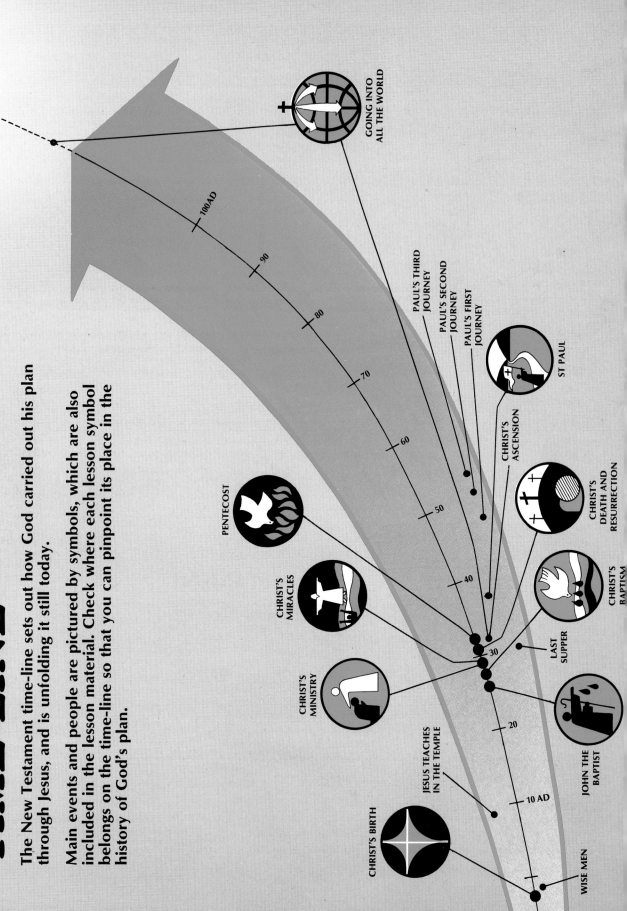

GOING INTO ALL THE WORLD

100AD

90

80

70

60

50

40

PAUL'S THIRD JOURNEY

PAUL'S SECOND JOURNEY

PAUL'S FIRST JOURNEY

ST PAUL

CHRIST'S ASCENSION

CHRIST'S DEATH AND RESURRECTION

PENTECOST

CHRIST'S MIRACLES

CHRIST'S BAPTISM

LAST SUPPER

CHRIST'S MINISTRY

30

20

JESUS TEACHES IN THE TEMPLE

10 AD

CHRIST'S BIRTH

JOHN THE BAPTIST

WISE MEN

17

Prepare the way!

Ugly walls and broken fences were being repaired; old roads were being re-surfaced; paint-brushes were out to give everything a quick face-lift. Finally, large posters began to appear with the message: WELCOME TO OUR TOWN. The town was getting ready for the visit of the Queen.
Why are many people glad to welcome a royal visitor?
Why do they specially prepare for the visit?

'The King is coming! Make the way ready for him!' This was the urgent message of John the Baptizer to the people of Israel.

John had a special part to play in God's great plan. God sent him as his messenger to tell his people that a new age was beginning. At last the promised Son of David, the Messiah for whom they had been waiting, was coming.

THE KING'S MESSENGER

There was something special about this messenger of the King. The story of his birth shows that God's power was at work.

One day, a priest called Zechariah was working in the temple in Jerusalem. Suddenly he saw an angel of the Lord, and was terrified. 'Your wife, Elizabeth, is going to have a baby', the heavenly messenger announced. 'You will call him John. He will be the prophet sent by God to prepare his people for the coming of the Lord.'

Zechariah was astonished. 'Surely this can't be true', he said. 'My wife and I are too old to have children.' 'God's word is sure', the angel declared, 'and because you have doubted it, you will not be able to speak until God's promise is fulfilled.' From that moment on, Zechariah lost his power to speak.

Some months later, the child was born — just as the angel had promised. Eight days after his birth, people gathered for the child's circumcision. At this ceremony, the baby boy was made a member of the people of Israel and given his name. The neighbours wanted him to be called Zechariah, like his father. But Zechariah asked for a writing tablet and wrote: 'His name is John!' Suddenly Zechariah could speak again, and broke into an inspired song about God's plan for this child:

66 *You, my child, will be called a prophet of the Most High God. You will go ahead of the Lord to prepare his road for him, to tell his people that they will be saved by having their sins forgiven. Our God is merciful and tender.* 99

'Who is this child, and what will he be?' the people wondered when they saw these signs of God's power at work.

BIBLE SEARCH
READ LUKE 1:67–80.

What promise had God made to his people?
How was God keeping his promises?
Talk about what was special about John as he grew up.

THE PROPHET OF THE LORD

God's power was with John in his work as the Lord's messenger. He grew up to be a mighty prophet, and the Holy Spirit was upon him. In the desert near the River Jordan, John lived close to God in prayer and meditation as he prepared for his great work. He lived a simple life, wearing a coat of camel's hair and a leather belt, and eating locusts and wild honey.

The day came when John began to speak the message God had given him:

The Lord is coming. The only way to get ready for him is to turn away from your sins. Be baptized here in the River Jordan so that you may be forgiven! Open your hearts to the coming King so that you may enter his kingdom.

People everywhere heard about this strange prophet God had sent, and they flocked out to the River Jordan to see him. When they heard his message, many of them were sorry for their sins, and were baptized for the forgiveness of their sins.

'Now live in a way which shows that you have really turned away from your sins and are ready for the King who is coming', John told them.

Some men became followers of John and lived with him in the desert. They helped John in his work as he kept preaching and waiting for the Messiah to be revealed. For these men, too, the big question was: 'Who is this King who is coming, and how shall we know him?'

BIBLE SEARCH
READ LUKE 3:1-17.

How did John prepare the way for the coming King?
Why did he baptize people?
What made his work for God so hard?

IMAGINARY INTERVIEW BETWEEN JOHN AND SOME PHARISEES WHO WERE SENT TO QUESTION HIM

Channel ISR Jerusalem reporting:

'John, you have received a lot of publicity. Who are you? Are you the Messiah?'

'I am not. He is so much greater than I that I am not even worthy to undo his shoelace. I am simply the one that God has sent to prepare the way for his coming.'

'Then who is this Messiah you keep talking about?'

'He is the Coming One, the Lord whom God will send to bring in the kingdom of God. You must turn from your sinful ways and get ready to welcome him.'

'Why do you call us sinners? We are the children of Abraham.'

'Don't be proud that you are the children of Abraham! You are like snakes. Your lives are crooked and full of evil. Don't you know that God is going to punish you?'

'Why are you baptizing people? Who gave you the authority?'

'God has sent me. Everyone needs to repent and get ready for the Lord's coming: soldiers, tax collectors, the common people — all of them. They must show by their lives that they are ready for the coming of the Saviour whom God has promised.'

THE MAIN POINTS AGAIN

- God sent John as his special prophet to prepare the way for the coming Messiah. John was really the last of the Old Testament prophets, but he saw the actual coming of the Christ and the dawning of the new age.

- John told the people to get ready for the coming King. Being prepared did not mean just being the descendants of Abraham; it meant having the right relationship with God by repenting of their sins and receiving God's forgiveness.

KEY BIBLE PASSAGE   MATTHEW 11:7–15

How does Jesus describe John and his work? Talk about why he was such a great prophet. How was he especially blessed?

THIS IS MEANT FOR US TODAY

1. John has an important message for God's people today. He calls on us all to repent and to let Jesus be our King.

   Read Luke 3:3–5.

   > Why do we need to repent of our sins every day? How can we show that we are sorry for our sins?

2. Each year God's people prepare for the coming of Christ the Lord during a special season of the church-year. This season is called Advent.

   > Talk about the meaning of Advent, and how the Church uses this time to prepare for Christ's coming.

WORSHIP

Read Psalm 24 responsively.

A LITANY PRAYER:
Help us to turn away from sin and to serve you daily:
  Come, Lord Jesus, and live in our hearts.
Help us to trust your promise that you will come again and give us eternal life:
  Come, Lord Jesus, and live in our hearts.

Scripture references: Matthew 3:1–12; Mark 1:1–8; Luke 1:5–25, 57–80; 3:1–17.

FAMILY EXTRA

Ask members of your family to help you make this poster. Display it in your home.

For a devotion, read Matthew 3:1–6. For a prayer, read (or sing) the hymn 'O come, O come, Emmanuel'.

PREPARE THE WAY OF THE LORD

MORE TO DO

1. Prepare a 'Jesse Tree' as a class project. Discuss what this is, and how you could illustrate it.

2. Read the story of John's birth in Luke 1:5–25, 57–80. Discuss what was special about the birth of this child, and what Old Testament prophecies were fulfilled with his coming.

3. Members of the class could each choose one of the books of the New Testament, read the introduction in the Good News Bible, and report on the book back to the class.

4. Read Luke 1:1–3 and John 20:30,31 and discuss why the New Testament was written.

5. Read more about John the Baptizer and his work: Luke 3:1–17; John 1:19–28.

A child is born

18

It was Christmas Eve. The Sunday-school children were singing a carol as they presented the Christmas program:

'I know God loves me, In love redeems me;
I know God loves me, For he is love:
Therefore I say again, I know God loves me,
I know God loves me, For God is love.

'He sent me Jesus, My faithful Saviour,
He sent me Jesus And set me free:'

As they heard the children telling the Christmas story, all in the church seemed very happy, and gladly joined in the singing.

Why do Christians all over the world celebrate the birthday of Jesus?

What makes us so happy at this celebration?

The crucial time had come — the time for God to take the most important step in his whole saving plan. It was time for that special Person to come who would bring blessing on the whole world.

But who would this Person be, since no sinful human being could save the world? God did something truly amazing: He himself came down to earth to be born as the Saviour. The Son of God became the Son of Man.

This is the most amazing thing about God's plan. What God had in mind all the time was the secret which he revealed at the first Christmas.

CHOSEN

A young woman called Mary was sitting in her home in the little town of Nazareth in Galilee. She belonged to the family of King David. She was a God-fearing young woman who longed for God to send the Messiah to save his people.

Suddenly, the room was filled with dazzling light. The angel Gabriel had come to bring her a message from God: 'Peace be with you, Mary. God has greatly blessed you. He has chosen you to be the mother of a baby boy. He will be a holy child, and you will call him Jesus. He will be the Son of God. He will be the king of David's line whom God has promised. He will be great, and his kingdom will never end.'

Mary was frightened. 'How can this be?' she asked. 'I'm not even married yet.' 'The Holy Spirit will cause you to have this child, and God's power will be on you', the angel explained.

Mary was amazed that God had chosen her — someone so lowly and unimportant. But she was thankful for the grace God had shown her. 'I am the Lord's servant', she said. 'May it happen as you said.'

If Mary had kept a diary, what might she have written in the months that followed?

MARY'S DIARY:

Today I arrived at cousin Elizabeth's house. She is having a special baby, too. When she greeted me, I felt so happy that I sang a song of praise to God. I think I will stay here with Elizabeth for about three months . . .

Joseph came to see me today when I came back to Nazareth. An angel has told him about the baby God has given me. We are going to get married straight away. God is truly looking after me! Now I will have someone to care for me . . .

Soon I will have my baby. But now we have to travel all the way down to Bethlehem. The Emperor Augustus in Rome has said that we must all go to the home town of our families to enrol in the census. It will be a hard journey, but I know no harm will come to me . . .

The most wonderful thing has happened! The baby God promised was born safely last night. He is beautiful! We are here in this cattle stable because there was no room in the inn. Yet the inn-keeper was kind to us. He has let us use this warm and sheltered place. I have laid the baby in the soft hay.

What God told me about this baby is surely true! Soon after he was born, some shepherds came here. They had been looking after their sheep when angels appeared, praising God and telling them the good news that the Saviour had been born. Just imagine! My baby is Christ the Lord! The shepherds were very happy and bowed before him. It is truly amazing. This baby is God's Son, yet he is born here in this cattle shed! . . .

It is a week now since the baby was born. Today he was circumcised, and we called him 'Jesus'. The angel told us to call him that because he is the Saviour . . .

Another amazing thing has happened! My baby is truly the Saviour-King! This evening some strange, richly-dressed men arrived to greet the baby. They came from the east. For months they had been following a bright star which told them that the King of the Jews had been born. The star led them to our house here at Bethlehem. They worshipped the little child as their Lord and King. They gave him rich gifts: gold and precious perfume. God is looking after us. Now we have all the money we need . . .

It has been a hard day today. Joseph suddenly made us pack up and leave. Wicked King Herod wants to kill the baby! He is jealous of him because Jesus is a king, so we are going to Egypt. We will live there as long as Herod is alive. It's strange to think that we are going to Egypt just like our forefather Jacob! I can't help wondering where all this will finally lead . . .

BIBLE SEARCH
READ LUKE 2:22–35.

Why did Mary take Jesus to the temple?
What did Simeon say about the baby?

JESUS GROWS UP

After Herod died, Joseph returned with Mary and Jesus to live in Nazareth. He continued his work as a carpenter. Jesus grew up with the blessing of God on him. He went to the synagogue school and studied the Old Testament. He lived quietly in Nazareth until he was about 30 years old.

BIBLE SEARCH
READ LUKE 2:41–50.

Why did Mary and Joseph take Jesus to Jerusalem?
Why did Jesus stay behind in the temple?
What did he tell his mother?

ACCORDING TO PLAN

- At the right time, God carried out his plan to save the world from sin, death, and the power of the devil.

- Only God could do what had to be done. God's own Son was born as a man to be the Saviour-King.

- Jesus was true man, born of the Virgin Mary. He was true God, Son of the Father from eternity.

- After a short time in Egypt, Jesus lived in Nazareth with Mary and Joseph until the time came for God to reveal him publicly as the One whom he had sent to be the Saviour.

KEY BIBLE PASSAGE   JOHN 1:9–14

St John tells us about the central fact in the history of the world.

What is so amazing about the birth of Jesus?
Why did God send the Messiah in such a humble way?
Which people recognized the true glory of the Saviour?

GOD'S PEOPLE TODAY

1. Christ was born to be **our** Saviour. Each Christmas we celebrate God's love in sending his Son to free us from sin and death.

Read Galatians 4:4.

Christ was born to be 'the man for all nations'. Why, then, was he born a Jew? How does Christmas show that God is **for us** and not against us?

2. At Christmas time, God's people are often asked to give money to help needy people.

Discuss whether your congregation has a special collection at that time.
Why are we asked to do this at Christmas time?

WORSHIP

Sing a Christmas carol.

Read Simeon's prayer responsively:

Now, Lord, you have kept your promise:
And you may let your servant go in peace.
With my own eyes I have seen your salvation:
Which you have prepared in the presence of all peoples;
A light to reveal your will to the Gentiles:
And bring glory to your people Israel. Amen.

Scripture references: Luke 1:26–56; 2; Matthew 1:18–25; 2.

WITH YOUR FAMILY

Ask members of your family which is their favourite Christmas carol, and why. Keep a list.

For a family devotion, read John 1:10–18. Read (or sing) one of the carols chosen by family members. Perhaps each person could share what Christmas means to him. As a closing prayer, use Simeon's words in Luke 2:29–32.

MORE CHALLENGES

1. Make sure your class time-line is up to date as you mark in the birth of Christ (about 4 BC).

2. God's plan to save the world depended on the birth of a baby — his own Son. How did God's plans in Old Testament times sometimes depend on the birth of 'special babies'? What was different about the birth of the Christ-child?

3. Did Jesus grow up just like any ordinary boy? Discuss this.

4. Talk to your grandparents or some elderly person about how they used to celebrate Christmas when they were children. Be ready to report to the class.

5. Just like the Israelites of old, Jesus came out of Egypt to live in Canaan, the land of promise. Read Matthew 2:14,15, and discuss why Matthew tells us this about Jesus.

S... r *service*

19

...ur profession and assurance, I set you apart to serve the ...missionary, in the name of the Father, and of the Son, and of ...pirit.'

...are the words a pastor speaks when commissioning ...one as a missionary. Then the whole congregation prays that ...will bless and help the missionary in his important work.

...*y does the Church have special services when a pastor is ...talled or a missionary commissioned?*

The heavenly Father was now ready to introduce Jesus to the people of Israel as the One whom he had sent. He publicly announced that Jesus was set apart for a special task. Jesus would carry out God's plan of rescue, and bring blessing to the whole world.

Set apart to carry out God's plan of rescue

THE FATHER'S WITNESS

One day, as John the Baptizer was preaching on the banks of the Jordan, he saw Jesus coming. Jesus asked John to baptize him, but John did not want to do this. 'You are much greater than I', he said. But Jesus told him, 'Baptize me, John. We must do all that my Father requires.'

After Jesus was baptized, he saw heaven opened, and the Holy Spirit coming down on him like a dove. Then a voice spoke from heaven: 'This is my own dear Son with whom I am pleased'.

In this way, God anointed his Son, Jesus, to be the Christ. He set him apart as his Servant to carry out his special work. The Holy Spirit gave him power to do all that his Father had sent him to do.

Now John knew that Jesus was the Holy One whom God had sent to be the Messiah. 'Look', he proclaimed, 'there is the Lamb of God who takes away the sin of the world.'

We are given the Holy Spirit who gives the power to be obedient to our "calling" or task.

BIBLE SEARCH
READ JOHN 1:29–34.

Why did John call Jesus the 'Lamb of God'?
How did John know that Jesus was the Son of God?

81

Just because we are set apart doesn't mean we are free from temptations, etc. and sin.

A TIME OF TESTING

After Jesus was baptized, the Holy Spirit led him out into the desert for a time of testing. There in the wilderness for forty days, Satan kept on tempting him. The devil tried to make Jesus doubt that he was really God's Son, and tried to make him act against his Father's will. But Jesus turned aside every temptation with the Word of God.

In one temptation, Satan offered to make Jesus king of the whole world if he would worship him. Jesus sternly commanded this lying tempter to go away. 'The Scripture says that you must worship the Lord your God and serve only him!', Jesus told Satan.

Jesus knew there was no easy way for him to gain the world for God. He had come to do his Father's will, and this meant he would have to take a hard path which would lead to trouble and suffering. Yet Jesus was determined to carry out all his Father wanted him to do.

Jesus beat Satan there in the desert. In his time of testing, he showed that he was mightier than the devil. Though Adam and Eve had fallen into sin when tempted, Jesus overcame the devil through the power of the Word of God. He trusted his Father's Word completely and obeyed him perfectly.

THE WORK HE HAD COME TO DO

BEGIN BY DOING

Jesus began his work in Galilee, preaching and teaching, healing the sick, and helping people in their troubles. Soon the news of the wonderful things he was doing spread everywhere.

One day, he returned to his home town of Nazareth. On the Saturday he went to the synagogue for worship. He stood up and read from the Old Testament the words of the prophet Isaiah:

BIBLE SEARCH
READ MATTHEW 4:1-11.

Long ago, God had led the Israelites through the waters of the Red Sea into the desert where they were tried and tested for 40 years. Now God's own Son went from the waters of the Jordan into the desert for 40 days of testing.

Why did the Holy Spirit lead Jesus out to be tempted?

What were the three temptations of Satan?

How did Jesus overcome the devil for us?

> 66 *The Spirit of the Lord is upon me, because he has chosen me to bring the good news to the poor.*
> *He has sent me to proclaim liberty to the captives and recovery of sight to the blind;*
> *to set free the oppressed and announce that the time has come when the Lord will save his people.* 99
>
> **Isaiah 61:1,2 as quoted in Luke 4:18**

After the reading, Jesus rolled up the scroll and said: 'Today what God has promised has come true'. In this way, Jesus announced that he was the great Servant God had sent to save his people. He had come to preach the good news of forgiveness, and to help all those in trouble. God had chosen him to be the Saviour of the world.

THESE ARE THE HEADLINES

- At Jesus' baptism, God publicly anointed him as the Christ who had come to be the Saviour. The Father declared that Jesus was his own Son, and gave him power to do his work.

- By being baptized, Jesus showed that he had come to be one with sinners and to help them in their trouble. He was the Lamb of God who would take away the sins of the world.

- Before he began his ministry, Jesus went through a time of testing. Adam and Eve had fallen into temptation, but Jesus overcame the power of Satan for all people.

- In the power of the Holy Spirit, Jesus began to preach and teach as God's Servant.

 **KEY BIBLE PASSAGE   LUKE 4:16–30**

Long ago, the prophets had spoken of the work which the special Servant of God would do.

What was the work for which Jesus was set apart?
Why did the people in Nazareth get so angry?
Why did Jesus' work lead to trouble and suffering?

THE MEANING FOR US

1. Jesus was set apart for service **for us**. All that he did, he did **for us** as our perfect Saviour — according to God's plan.

   > Read Hebrews 2:14–18.
   > What special work did Jesus come to do for us?
   > How are we blessed by his work today?

2. How are God's people today 'set apart for service'?
   Here are some ways we can work for God; talk about them, and think of other ways:

   > showing love in our families . . .
   > worshipping . . . witnessing . . . helping the needy . . .

FAMILY TIME

Get your family to help you make a mobile about Jesus, the Servant of God.

As a devotion, read Luke 4:14–21. Talk about some of the things Jesus did as God's Servant. For a prayer, read (or sing) the verses of the hymn below.

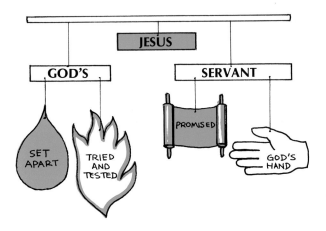

WORSHIP

Pray (or sing) these verses:

Take my life, and let it be
Consecrated, Lord, to thee;
Take my moments and my days,
Let them flow in ceaseless praise.

Take my voice, and let me sing
Always, only, for my king;
Take my lips, and let them be
Filled with messages from thee.

Take my will, and make it thine;
It shall be no longer mine.
Take my heart; it is thine own,
It shall be thy royal throne.

Take my love, my Lord, I pour
At thy feet its treasure-store.
Take myself, and I will be
Ever, only, all for thee.

MORE TO DO

1. Three of the Gospels tell us about the baptism of Jesus: Matthew 3:13–17; Mark 1:9–11; Luke 3:21,22. Choose one of these, and make a comic-strip version of the story.

2. Find the names of any pastors or missionaries who have come from your congregation. Find out where they are working. Pray for these people.

3. Talk about how God can use troubles and temptations to help us today. Discuss why Jesus' victory over Satan is so important for us.

4. Jesus is still working through his Church today. Find or write a prayer asking God to bless the work.

Bible references: Matthew 3:13–17; 4:1–11; Mark 1:9–13; Luke 3:21,22; 4:1–30.

JESUS' YEARS OF SPECIAL MINISTRY

For about three years Jesus carried on his ministry of preaching and healing. The Gospels tell us of his travels, but they do not say exactly how his various preaching tours fit together.

Jesus travelled throughout Galilee. He visited Jerusalem for several feasts of the Jews, and passed through Samaria. On one occasion, he journeyed into the land of Phoenicia. Toward the end of his ministry, he went to Judea and visited the regions east of the River Jordan, known as Perea. From there he returned to Jerusalem for his final ministry.

(The map shows the various places Jesus visited.)

Palestine
In the time of Christ

SCALE IN KILOMETRES

0   10   20   40   60   80

Scripture references for the journeys of Jesus:
Matthew 4:23; 9:35; 16:13; Mark 7:24; Luke 8:1,26; 17:11; John 2:13; 3:22; 4:3,4; 4:43; 5:1; 10:22,40; 11:17,18; 11:54; 12:1.

SYRIA

PHOENICIA

TYRE

CAESAREA PHILIPPI

GALILEE

PLAIN OF GENNESARET

CHORAZIN
CAPERNAUM
BETHSAIDA

SEA OF GALILEE

CANA

MAGDALA

NAZARETH

NAIN

GADARA

CAESAREA

RIVER JORDAN

SAMARIA

SYCHAR
JACOB'S WELL

SAMARIA

PEREA

MEDITERRANEAN SEA

JOPPA

EPHRAIM

JERICHO

BAPTISM OF JESUS

EMMAUS
JERUSALEM
BETHANY

BETHLEHEM

GAZA

DEAD SEA

JUDEA

EGYPT

FOUR PICTURES OF THE SAVIOUR

The four Gospels in the New Testament tell us about Jesus' ministry as the Saviour. Each of them tells the story from a different point of view. Together, they help us to get a deeper understanding of Jesus as a person and of the work he did for us. Here are some of the emphases you will find in the Gospels:

ACCORDING TO MATTHEW

JESUS IS THE LONG-AWAITED MESSIAH, WHO:

- fulfils God's promises to his Old Testament people;
- teaches about God's kingdom and his will for those who follow him;
- dies for our sins and, after he has risen again, sends out his followers to tell the Good News to all people.

ACCORDING TO MARK

JESUS IS THE STRONG DELIVERER SENT BY GOD, WHO:

- has power and authority over sickness, nature, demons, and death;
- dies to set us free from sin, and conquers death by rising triumphantly on the third day.

GOOD NEWS ABOUT JESUS

ACCORDING TO LUKE

JESUS IS THE LOVING SAVIOUR OF ALL, WHO:

- reaches out to help the troubled and outcasts;
- teaches about his Father's love and forgiveness;
- lays down his life for sinners, and rises again to show that he has won the victory.

ACCORDING TO JOHN

JESUS IS THE TRUE SON OF GOD, WHO:

- became a man and lived among us as the Saviour who reveals his Father's love;
- shows his glory by his works and through his suffering and dying for us;
- conquers death so that all who believe in him may be his friends for ever.

20

The Kingdom is here

Little Jenny was excited when she set out to see the Queen on her visit to her city. But when she came home, she seemed rather disappointed: 'Mum, she looked quite ordinary — just like you!' When her mother showed her a picture of the Queen in her royal robes, with a crown on her head and a sceptre in her hand, Jenny asked: 'Why doesn't she always look like that?'

What do you think her mother answered?

'What's happening here?' the people of Galilee began to ask one another excitedly when they heard Jesus' preaching and saw his powerful miracles.

Jesus' message to the people gave them the explanation. 'I've got good news for you', he said. 'God has come to rule over you. His kingdom is coming to you. Turn away from your sins, and believe the Good News.'

WHAT KIND OF KING?

This was great news! Did this mean that things would now be as they were in the 'good old days' of Moses and King David, when God used to rule his people and defeat their enemies?, the people wondered. 'Perhaps this Jesus will be our King who will drive out the Romans and make us a strong nation again.'

But something puzzled the people. Jesus did not look like a king, and he did not act like a king. He did not gather an army to fight; he did not show the power and glory of an earthly king. He looked so ordinary, so humble. Instead of using royal titles, he often called himself mysteriously 'the Son of Man'.

This was all according to God's plan. God was not going to rule over his people with earthly power and glory, but with his love and mercy and forgiveness. He had sent his Son, Jesus, to set people free from the sin, misery, and death which Adam and Eve had brought into the world.

TEACHING ABOUT THE KINGDOM

To help the Jews understand the truth about God and his kingdom, Jesus taught many things about his loving rule. He taught in many different ways. Often he used parables. (A parable is a story or illustration from real life which has a deeper meaning and teaches a truth.)

BIBLE SEARCH
READ LUKE 17:20,21.

What kind of kingdom were the Pharisees expecting?

What kind of kingdom was coming with Jesus?

These two parables of Jesus tell us what KIND OF KING GOD IS . . .

A young man left home and travelled to a country far away. There he wasted the money his father had given him, living a wild, sinful life. Finally, he had no money left, and great trouble and hardship came on him. He got a job looking after pigs, and was so hungry that he even wanted to eat their food. Now he realized how wicked he had been. He decided to go back to his father, tell him how sorry he was, and ask his forgiveness. But how would his father receive him?

His father gladly welcomed him back, and even gave a party to celebrate. This made the boy's older brother jealous. His father had never given him a feast like that! But his father told him how glad they should be that his brother had come home again. 'He was dead, but now he is alive. He was lost, but now he has been found' (Luke 15:11–32).

God is a King like this loving father. He receives and forgives people, not because they deserve it, but because he is merciful. He will always receive those who turn to him for forgiveness and help.

Once a king prepared a wedding feast for his son. When everything was ready, he sent out his servants to tell the guests to come. But they began to make all kinds of excuses, and refused to come. The king was angry. He sent his servants to bring people in from the streets — all kinds of people, good and bad. In this way the wedding feast was filled with guests (Luke 14:15–24).

God wants people to be in his kingdom, even the lowliest. He wants them to enjoy his love and blessing. There is room for all. But people who don't want to be under God's rule will miss out on his blessings.

Some of the important things Jesus taught about LIVING UNDER THE RULE OF GOD . . .

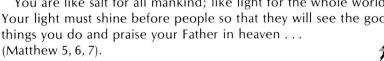

Don't worry about your life. Look at the birds and the flowers. See how God cares even for them. He will certainly take care of you. You can trust him . . .

You have heard what was said of old . . . but now I tell you:
Love your enemies; don't try to get revenge;
don't be angry with others; forgive other people.
Be holy and pure, like your heavenly father . . .

You are like salt for all mankind; like light for the whole world. Your light must shine before people so that they will see the good things you do and praise your Father in heaven . . .
(Matthew 5, 6, 7).

BIBLE SEARCH
READ LUKE 10:25–37.

Who is our neighbour?
Why is showing love to others the most
important rule for people in God's kingdom?

Two other parables Jesus told about the Kingdom . . .

A man found a treasure hidden in the field. He was so happy that he sold everything he had so that he could buy that field (Matthew 13:44).

To enter God's kingdom and become one of his people is the greatest blessing anyone can receive.

A man built his house on sand. When a flood came the house was destroyed. A wise man built his house on rock. No flood could hurt that house! (Matthew 7:24–27).

The wise person will build his life on the teaching of Jesus. Then he will be able to stand firm in all the troubles of life, for God is on his side.

BIBLE SEARCH
READ LUKE 7:16;
JOHN 7:40;
MATTHEW 17:5.

How did Jesus fulfil God's promise to send a
great prophet? (See Deuteronomy 18:15.)
Why did Jesus' teaching amaze people?
How did it challenge them?

THESE ARE THE MAIN POINTS

- Jesus came to set up God's rule. He did this by bringing God's love to people through his words and actions.

- Those people who repented of their sins and believed Jesus' good news came into God's kingdom.

- Jesus taught many things about the kingdom, and gave people the true Word of God. He was the great prophet whom God had promised to send.

KEY BIBLE PASSAGE   MARK 1:14,15,36,39

Jesus' special ministry was to bring people under God's loving rule.
What kind of king was Jesus? How was he different from other kings?

GOD'S PEOPLE TODAY

1. God's people today are glad to have God rule over them and to belong to his kingdom.

   > Read Colossians 1:11–14.
   > From what has God rescued us?
   > How does God set us free?

2. Jesus is **our** great prophet, or teacher. His Word brings us God's love and helps us to live as God's people (see Hebrews 1:11).

   How could Jesus' teaching help us:
   . . . when we feel depressed, or rejected?
   . . . when we begin to worry?
   . . . when we begin to feel confused about life?

WORSHIP

Dear Jesus, thank you for making us the children of God. Help us to live as those who belong to God's kingdom, and to show that you are our King. Hear us for your love's sake. Amen.

The four Gospels are full of Jesus' teaching. Here are some of the main sections from Matthew and Luke: Matthew 5; 6; 7; 10:24–39; 13; 18; 19; Luke 11; 12; 13; 14–16.

THE FAMILY TOGETHER

Make this poster as a family project. Feature the words of Jesus, called 'the golden rule'.

For a devotion, read Matthew 5:1–12. Family members could take turns in reading the verses. Finally, read vv 24–27 and close with the Lord's Prayer.

MORE TO DO

1. Study the Sermon on the Mount (Matthew 5, 6, 7) as a class project. Work out brief summaries of the sections of this sermon and write them on posters to display around the class.

2. More than 40 parables of Jesus are recorded in the Gospels. Choose one of them for illustrating with drawings and a suitable title. Display your drawings in the church.

3. Make a short play of one of the parables, such as the Prodigal Son (Luke 15:11–32), the Good Samaritan (Luke 10:25–37), or the Unmerciful Servant (Matthew 18:21–35), and act it out in class.

4. Find some of Jesus' best-known sayings: Matthew 7:12; 10:39; 19:30; 22:37–39; Mark 10:14,15.

5. Jesus taught about many aspects of our life. Choose one of the following topics, and discover what Jesus says about it:
. . . money: Matthew 19:23–26
. . . marriage and divorce: Matthew 19:3–9
. . . what makes a person unclean: Mark 7:14–23
. . . the Sabbath: Mark 2:23–28

Signs of the Kingdom

Thousands of people live in complete poverty on the streets of Calcutta without a home of their own. Many of them are sick and suffer from terrible diseases, but have no money to get help. A Catholic nun, called Mother Teresa, works among these 'poorest of the poor' and cares for them in their trouble. She does her work for the love of Jesus and to help the suffering.

Why does Mother Teresa work among these people?
How is her work a sign of God's care for the sick?

God's great plan was to save people from sin and all its evil effects on their bodies and souls. The miracles and wonders which Jesus performed, setting people free from sickness, suffering, and death, were signs that God was carrying out his plan through Jesus. They showed that God's kingdom had come. Jesus' mighty deeds were God's loving rule at work.

SIGNS OF HIS LOVE

By his loving deeds to help the sick and the dying, Jesus showed God's concern for people in their bodily need.

Let us imagine how the newspapers might have reported some of Jesus' miracles . . .

BIBLE SEARCH
READ MATTHEW 4:23-25.
Why did Jesus heal the sick?
Why could he heal them?

Capernaum Journal

PARALYSED MAN HEALED

An amazing scene took place in Capernaum today. Jesus of Nazareth was teaching in a house when friends brought a paralysed man on his bed to be healed. Witnesses report that, when these people couldn't get in the door, they let the bed down in front of Jesus through an opening in the roof. Jesus' reaction was surprising. He simply told the sick man that his sins were forgiven. This made the teachers of the law who were in the room very angry. 'No man has power to forgive sins', they said. But Jesus did not argue with them. He calmly told them he would prove that he had authority to forgive sins. Then, turning to the sick man, he told him to get up and go home. To everyone's astonishment the man was instantly cured and walked out of the house.

'Praise God!' Simon Peter commented to our reporter. 'There is no doubt that Jesus has the authority of God himself!'

DEAD GIRL ALIVE AGAIN

Tuesday

A young village girl who died yesterday is enjoying life at home with her parents today! Astounding as this may seem, it is the simple truth.

The 12-year-old daughter of the local synagogue leader, Jairus, collapsed and died yesterday from a serious illness which failed to respond to any medical treatment.

Reliable report that the miraculous recovery happened when the visiting teacher, Jesus of Nazareth, brought the girl back to life. They say that Jesus simply entered the dead girl's room, took her hand, and commanded her to get up. She was immediately alive again.

There seems no doubt that the amazing power of this man backs up his strange and challenging preaching.

JERICHO NEWS

Friday

Blind Bartimaeus, the beggar, can see again. He was cured today by the teacher called Jesus, as he passed through our town. Correspondents all around the country report similar miracles and mighty works. Bartimaeus is convinced that this man is the great Son of David whom God promised to send. If he is correct, the Messiah has truly come and the kingdom of God is at hand!

SIGNS OF SATAN'S OVERTHROW

By curing people possessed by demons, Jesus showed that Someone mightier than Satan had come with God's own authority to destroy the devil's power and bring in God's kingdom.

BIBLE SEARCH
READ LUKE 7:11–17.

Why did Jesus raise the young man?
What was Jesus teaching by his miracles of healing?

GERASA TIMES

Monday

MADMAN CURED

BEFORE   **AFTER**

It is safe again to go near the caves on the shore of Lake Galilee. The devil-possessed man who terrorised that area has been cured. When Jesus arrived by boat today, this madman met him and began to scream, 'Jesus, Son of the most high God, don't punish me, I beg you!' Jesus simply commanded the evil spirits to leave him. They appeared to enter a large herd of pigs nearby, which rushed down the slope and were drowned. The madman is now completely well again. He claims that Jesus is truly the Messiah who was to come. But many residents don't want anything to do with this teacher. They blame him for the loss of their pigs, and told him to leave.

SIGNS OF GOD'S POWER

By the mighty works which Jesus performed, he showed his power over the forces of nature.

'Who is this man?', his disciples asked when they experienced his amazing power: to stop a raging storm with a few words, to walk on water, to feed a large crowd with a few loaves and fishes, to turn water into wine.

By these signs of his power, Jesus showed that all things were subject to the kingly rule of God.

BIBLE SEARCH
READ LUKE 11:14-23.

How did some people explain Jesus' miracles?
How did his miracles point to the kingdom of God?

BIBLE SEARCH
Read about some of Jesus' nature miracles:
MARK 6:30-44 Jesus feeds a hungry crowd.

MARK 4:35-41 Jesus stops a storm.
What was Jesus teaching people by these miracles?

JOHN 2:1-11 Jesus changes water into wine. The time of joy and blessing promised in the kingdom of God was coming through Jesus. How did this miracle show this?

HERE ARE THE MAIN POINTS

- Jesus' miracles were the sign that the kingdom of God had come through him. They revealed his glory as the Son of God.

- Jesus' miracles showed that:
  God's love and power were present in Jesus, reaching out to help the suffering and afflicted;
  Jesus had God's own authority in his teaching;
  Jesus had power over Satan, and had come to save people from Satan's slavery;
  God was in control of all things, even the forces of nature, for the welfare of his people.

KEY BIBLE PASSAGE   MATTHEW 11:2-6

The promises of God were coming true in Jesus.

Why did John have doubts about Jesus being the Messiah?
How did the signs Jesus did point to the coming of the kingdom?

FOR US TODAY

1. God's people today also face sickness and death, and have to struggle against the power of Satan. But Jesus has proved to us that God is on our side to help and protect us.

   Read Romans 8:31–39.

   > Talk about some of the things which might alarm or frighten us.
   > Why can none of these things separate us from God's love?
   > Why can we be sure of this?

2. Talk about how God is helping us physically today: through medical science; through good diet and hygiene; other ways . . .

3. Jesus wants his people to help others in need.

   Read Galatians 6:10.

   > Why should God's people try to help others, as Mother Teresa does?
   > Discuss how you could help someone who is sick or in trouble.

WORSHIP

Dear Jesus, thank you for showing us your love and your power to help us when we are sick or in trouble. Thank you for all the ways you help us today. We gladly trust you to care for us in trouble, to heal us when we are sick, and to protect us day by day. In your name we pray. Amen.

Scripture references: Matthew 9:1–8; 14:22–32; Mark 5:21–43; 6:30–43; 10:46–52; Luke 8:22–25; John 2:1–11.

WITH YOUR FAMILY

As a family, decide to visit someone who is sick or in need. Talk about various ways you would help this person.

Read Matthew 4:23–25 and then choose one of Jesus' miracles to read. Talk about why Jesus cured the sick and how he still heals us today. Close with a prayer for the sick and for doctors and nurses.

MORE TO DO

1. The Gospels record about 40 miracles Jesus performed. One of his best-known is the raising of Lazarus. Read about this in John 11:33–44. Discuss what this miracle teaches us about Jesus.

2. Many people in Palestine were possessed by evil spirits, called demons. Talk about this. The evil spirits recognized the power of God in Jesus, and often cried out that he was the Son of God. Read Luke 4:41. Why did Jesus not want the witness of demons? Read how Jesus cured a boy possessed by a demon in Mark 9:17–27.

3. Unbelieving people asked Jesus to perform a special miracle. Read Matthew 12:38–42. Why would Jesus not do this miracle? What great sign would he give?

4. As a class, visit a hospital or elderly citizens' home to encourage those who are sick.

5. Choose one of the miracles of Jesus. Prepare an imaginary interview of the person cured by Jesus. Record it on cassette to play to the class.

Called to be disciples

In 155 AD, Polycarp, Bishop of Smyrna, died as a martyr during a persecution of Christians. When the Roman commander challenged him: 'Worship Caesar or die!', Polycarp replied: 'Eighty-six years I have served Christ, and he never did me wrong. How can I speak evil of Christ my King who saved me?' So he was tied to a stake and burnt.

Why was Polycarp willing to die for Jesus?
Why is it sometimes hard for us to be his disciples?

[handwritten annotations:]
Bros { Simon Peter
{ Andrew
Bro. { James
{ John
Philip
Bartholomew
Thomas
Matthew
James
Thaddeus the Zealot
Simon (from Canaan)
Judas Iscariot

 People everywhere were talking about Jesus. He was famous, and great crowds followed him for various reasons. Some were just curious; some thought he must be the Messiah, and hoped he would free them from the Romans and give them plenty. Others thought more deeply about his teaching and how God was at work through him.

As Jesus went throughout the land, he called on people to become his true followers. God was working in the hearts of some who came to believe in Jesus and looked for God to fulfil his plans through him. At Jesus' call, some left everything to follow him as his disciples. Disciples were people who learned from their master and teacher. Jesus taught much about what it meant to be **his** disciple. He wanted his followers to know clearly just what this involved.

In the following imaginary dialogues, we learn something about what it was like to be a disciple of Jesus:

THE COST OF BEING A DISCIPLE:

Jesus speaks to a man who wants to become his follower:

Benjamin ● Lord, I want to be your disciple!

Jesus ● *Following me is not easy, Benjamin. Do you realize what it will cost you? Only a fool starts building a tower without first working out what it will cost.*

Benjamin ● Master, I'll follow you, whatever it costs!

Jesus ● *If you want to be my disciple, you must say No to yourself, and give yourself completely to God and his kingdom.*

Benjamin ● I know following you won't be easy, Lord. But I'm sure that God has sent you, and I want to be your disciple.

Jesus ● *Follow me, then, and learn from me to give yourself to God and to love and serve others. My heavenly Father will help and bless you, and you will be in his kingdom.*

BIBLE SEARCH
READ LUKE 9:57–62.

Why did Jesus answer the way he did?

All kinds of people were attracted to Jesus. Some were important people. Others were people he had helped in trouble. This is how Nicodemus, a leader among the Pharisees, might have talked with Mary Magdalene, from whom Jesus had driven out demons.

Nicodemus ● Jesus must surely be a prophet sent by God! You believe that, don't you, Mary? Otherwise you wouldn't follow him as you do.

Mary ● I know that God is with him. He set me free from the power of demons. Now I try to show my thanks by helping him every way I can. He's the most loving person I've ever met.

Nicodemus ● Yes. He was a real friend to me that night I visited him. But what he says disturbs me. 'You must be born again', he told me.

Mary ● He challenges us all with his teaching. Do you want to be his disciple, too, Nicodemus?

Nicodemus ● It wouldn't be easy for me. Many of the Jewish leaders hate Jesus. Yet I'm sure God has sent him.

Voice of Jesus ● *Happy are you when people persecute you for being my followers. Come to me, all of you who are tired from carrying heavy loads, and I will give you rest.*

Jesus chose 12 men to be his special friends and helpers. He trained them to be his missionaries to help spread the Good News of the kingdom. Here some of the disciples speak about what it means to follow him.

James ● So, the Master has called you to follow him too, Matthew, has he? Life isn't always easy for us, following him around the country, away from home. But just being with him is worth it.

Matthew ● I couldn't say No when he told me to follow him. There's something wonderful about him. I'm sure God has sent him. But fancy him choosing me — a tax collector!

John ● We're all just ordinary people. He could have chosen great and important people, but he picked us. I was fishing when he called me to follow him. 'You will be fishers of men', he told us.

Andrew ● I'm beginning to understand what he meant. He wants us to help him in his work of showing people God's love and bringing them into his kingdom.

Thomas ● That's why he keeps on teaching us about his Father and his rule over us. It's wonderful to think of God as our loving Father. Jesus told us to call him 'Abba' just as though we were his little children.

Matthew ● There's so much I have to learn! A whole new life lies ahead! What a challenge to be a disciple of Jesus!

BIBLE SEARCH
READ LUKE 11:1-13.

What did Jesus teach them to pray for? Try to write the Lord's Prayer in your own words.

Imagine the scene as Jesus sends out his disciples to be missionaries.

SCENE I:

Jesus ● *I'm sending you out to the towns and villages around about as my missionaries. Go in my name and with my authority.*

Peter ● What shall we tell people, Master?

Jesus ● *Tell them to turn to my Father for mercy, and he will gladly accept them as his people. Show them what it means to have God as King and to live as his people.*

John ● What will we need to take with us, Jesus?

Jesus ● *You don't need to take anything. God will look after you. Some people will gladly hear your message and open their homes to you.*

James ● What shall we do, Lord, if we meet sick people, or people possessed by demons?

Jesus ● *I give you power over the demons. Drive them out, and heal the sick. The time of God's loving rule has come.*

SCENE II: The disciples return, happy and excited, from their journey.

Peter ● Lord, we preached the Good News and healed the sick, just as you told us. Many were glad to hear the message. Even the demons obeyed us when we spoke in your name.

Jesus ● *You are glad to do these things in my name. Be even more glad that you belong to my heavenly Father and have eternal life with him. I tell you, you'll do even greater things for me. You'll see the power of Satan broken and many people coming into the kingdom of God.*

BIBLE SEARCH

READ MATTHEW 10:1-4
to find out who were the men whom Jesus called to be his 12 disciples.

The people of Israel were formed from the 12 tribes of Israel. Why did Jesus choose 12 disciples?

THESE ARE THE MAIN POINTS

● Many people wanted to follow Jesus. He taught clearly what it meant to be his disciples: giving first place to Jesus, and living for God's kingdom.

● God led some people sincerely to believe in Jesus and to accept his message about the kingdom. They became Jesus' true followers.

● Jesus chose 12 disciples to be his special helpers. God planned to use them as messengers through whom he would gather in his people of the New Testament.

KEY BIBLE PASSAGE   **MATTHEW 16:24-28**

Being Jesus' disciple meant accepting him as Lord and living according to his teaching.

What was necessary if a person wanted to follow Jesus?
What blessings would this bring?

THE MEANING FOR US

1. We who are disciples of Jesus face the challenge of living as his followers.

   Read John 15:11–17.
   How can you tell today if someone is Christ's disciple?
   List some characteristics of those who follow him.

2. Give examples of how you could show that you were a follower of Jesus:

   . . . at home . . . at school . . . with your friends.

WORSHIP

RESPONSIVE PRAYER:
We are your disciples, Lord Jesus, and are called by your name:
   Help us, Lord, to walk in your way.
Give us strength to follow you in all we do, think, or say:
   Help us, Lord, to walk in your way.
Make us glad to serve you and to point others to you as the Saviour:
   Help us, Lord, to walk in your way.

Some of the main references to Jesus and his disciples: Matthew 16:24–28; Luke 14:25–34; 9:57–62; John 3; Luke 5:1–11; Matthew 9; Matthew 10:1–24; Luke 10:1–24.

WITH YOUR FAMILY

Quiz the members of your family to see if they know the names of the 12 disciples. Read the above dialogue between Nicodemus and Mary to your family, followed by Matthew 16:24–28. You could use the hymn 'O Jesus, I have promised' as a prayer.

MORE CHALLENGES

1. How did Jesus challenge these people to be his followers: Matthew 4:18–22, Luke 5:27,28; Matthew 19:16–22? Talk about how their lives were affected by Jesus' call.

2. Make a poster, setting out Jesus' rules for living as his disciples: Matthew 22:37–40. Write out some ways you can be a better disciple.

3. Jesus used the illustration of a vine bearing fruit to teach what it means to be his disciple. Read John 15:1–10. Make a drawing of this illustration. On the grapes, write in some of the good things we can do as disciples.

4. Here are some well-known disciples from more recent times: David Livingstone; Dietrich Bonhoeffer; Father Damien. Find out something about them and report to the class.

5. Jesus told a parable about the way people reacted to his teaching. Read Matthew 13:3–9. Discuss the way various people respond to Jesus today.

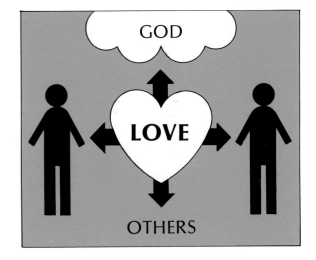

Seeking the lost

Civil war had broken out in a country. The bombing and shelling were causing death and destruction. To escape the fighting, thousands of people fled into a neighbouring country.

But now they were homeless, and many of them were injured and starving. The Red Cross came to the aid of these refugees. They set up camps, and provided food, clothing, and medicine. The sign of the Red Cross brought new hope for these outcasts.

What is the purpose of the organization known as the 'Red Cross'?
Why was a cross chosen as a symbol of this organization?

THE FRIEND OF SINNERS

God is the friend of outcasts and sinners. He reaches out to help them in their trouble. No one is too lowly or too sinful to come into his kingdom. There is room for all. So Jesus invited all to turn to him for help and forgiveness.

As Jesus travelled about with his disciples, teaching and healing, he showed this tender love of God. He welcomed and helped the worst of sinners.

In some of his most beautiful parables, Jesus pictured this love of his heavenly Father for those who have gone astray. 'God is glad over one sinner who repents', Jesus said. God is like the caring shepherd who left his 99 sheep to go looking for the one which was lost, and who was glad when he found it. God is like a woman who cleaned out her whole house looking for the silver coin she had lost, and who gave a party when she found it.

Lowly people, those who were despised and rejected by the proud and respectable, were often the most thankful for the Good News Jesus brought about his Father's love for them.

THE SAVIOUR OF THE LOST

One day Jesus went to a feast given by Matthew (whom he had called to be his disciple). Matthew was looked down upon by most people because he collected taxes for the Roman government. Matthew's friends were at the feast also — outcasts and sinners like himself. When some of the Pharisees saw Jesus sharing the company of such people, they were disgusted.

'It's the sick who need a doctor', Jesus told these Pharisees. 'You may think you don't need God's mercy and forgiveness. But I have come to help those who know they are sinners, and want God to forgive them.'

REACHING OUT IN LOVE

On one occasion, as Jesus journeyed through
Samaria, he met a Samaritan woman drawing water
from a well at Sychar. When Jesus asked her for a
drink, she was amazed. (Jews despised Samaritans and
would not talk to them.) But Jesus wanted to lead this
woman into God's kingdom. He talked to her about
the 'living water' which he had come to bring. By this
he meant the love and forgiveness which God gave to
all those who entered his kingdom.

Jesus' words had a deep effect on this woman.
Could this be the promised Messiah?, she wondered.
She went back to the town, and brought others to
hear him. Many of these Samaritans believed what
Jesus taught.

Once again, Jesus had shown that he was the
Saviour, reaching out to help the outcasts and those
despised by other people.

LOVE FOR THE OUTCASTS

One day, a Pharisee named Simon invited Jesus to
his place for dinner. As they were eating, a sinful
woman entered and stood at Jesus' feet, weeping
because of her evil life. She poured a jar of expensive
perfume over his feet and dried them with her hair.
Simon was horrified that Jesus let such a wicked
woman touch him.

'Simon', Jesus told him firmly, yet kindly, 'when I
came to your home, you did not specially welcome
me. But this woman has done this for me because she
loves and trusts in me.' Then, turning to the woman
he said: 'Your sins are forgiven. Go in peace. Your
faith has saved you.'

ZACCHAEUS THE TAX COLLECTOR

Everyone in Jericho knew that Zacchaeus was a
thief. Most of the townspeople despised him because
he was a tax collector. As Jesus was going into Jericho
one day, he saw Zacchaeus up in the tree which he
had climbed to get a better look at Jesus as he passed
by. Jesus also knew that Zacchaeus was a thief, but he
called out: 'Come down, Zacchaeus. I'm coming to
your place for dinner today!' Zacchaeus was
astonished. Fancy this famous teacher wanting to eat
with him!

During the meal, as Jesus talked about God and his
kingdom, Zacchaeus began to feel very sorry for the
wrong he had done. He wanted God's forgiveness. 'I
will give back all the money I have stolen', he told
Jesus.

BIBLE SEARCH
READ LUKE 18:9–14.

Talk about the meaning of this parable.

Discuss why many outcasts went into the
kingdom of God rather than people like the
Pharisees.

Jesus, glad that Zacchaeus had turned back to God, said: 'The Son of Man has come to seek and to save the lost'.

GIVING HIS LIFE AS A RANSOM

Jesus told his disciples that they could have true life through him. He said: 'I came not to be served, but to serve, and to give my life as a ransom for many'. In this way, Jesus was preparing his disciples for the great sacrifice he would offer as the Lamb of God to take away the sins of the world.

BIBLE SEARCH
READ MARK 10:13–16.

Why was Jesus angry with his disciples?

Why were children important to him?

GETTING THE POINT

- God's plan was to save the whole world through his Son. Jesus showed this seeking, winning love of God by reaching out to help all people in their sin and trouble.

- Jesus was the special friend of the weak and the troubled, the lowly and the outcasts.

- All who turned to Jesus for help received God's love and forgiveness. But Jesus could not help proud people who did not want him to be their Saviour.

KEY BIBLE PASSAGE   MATTHEW 9:35–38

The love of Jesus moved him to action. In every way possible, he helped people in their need.

How did Jesus reach out to help people?
Why were many more workers needed for the kingdom of God?
Whom did Jesus mean by these workers?

In the Old Testament, God's special name was 'I AM WHO I AM' (the Lord). This name told of his love and care for his people. Jesus often referred to himself as the One in whom this love of God was fulfilled.

Think about the following I AM statements of Jesus from the Gospel of John, and talk about their meaning.

I AM the good shepherd (10:11).

I AM the light of the world (8:12).

I AM the door (10:9).

I AM the way, the truth, and the life (14:6).

I AM the true vine (15:1).

I AM the bread of life (6:35).

I AM the resurrection and the life (11:25).

GOD'S PEOPLE TODAY

1. No matter how weak and sinful we are, we can be sure Jesus is **for us**. He has come to help us all today in our trouble and need.

   Read Matthew 11:28–30.
   Whom does Jesus want to come to him?
   What does he promise them?

2. God's people today try to follow Jesus' example.

   Read James 2:1–5.
   Why should we care especially for the lowly and the outcasts?

WORSHIP

Pray this litany. Work out more sentences to say. Give the same response after each one:

When we have fallen into sin:
   Help us, dear Jesus.
When we are weak and discouraged:
   Help us, dear Jesus.
When we . . .

FAMILY TIME

Find pictures of Jesus as the Good Shepherd, the Light of the World, or similar illustrations. Use the pictures at a family devotion. Read the I AM sayings of Jesus (see above), and let family members say what these mean for them. Close with the hymn 'Come unto me, ye weary'.

MORE CHALLENGES

1. Read Jesus' parables about the lost coin, the lost sheep, the lost son (Luke 15). Make a poster of each parable, with a suitable caption, for display in class.

2. Jesus came to help all kinds of people. Read Luke 10:38–42; John 3:1–3; 8:1–11, and find out whom he is helping and how.

3. Many people did not want Jesus' help. Often these were the rich and important people. Read Matthew 19:16–30. Discuss how Jesus tried to help this young man, and why he turned away from Jesus.

4. Talk about the various ways your congregation reaches out to help people in need.

5. As a class project, plan to help someone in trouble in your community.

Scripture references: Luke 5:27–32; 7:36–50; 15:1–10; 19:1–10; John 4:5–42.

A time for decision

People who condemn evil and injustice in society and work for reform are often hated . . .
People who make important discoveries which threaten accepted ideas are often rejected.

Who were: Florence Nightingale . . . Emily Pankhurst . . . Martin Luther King?
Why were they persecuted for their work?

'I have not come to bring peace, but a sword', Jesus once said. He meant that people were being forced to decide whether they were for him or against him. His Good News about the kingdom was stirring up much opposition. Many people rejected Jesus and became his enemies.

Jesus knew that the work he had come to do for his Father would cause some people to hate and persecute him. But he was God's obedient Servant, and did all that his Father asked of him. Even his suffering was according to God's plan, through which he would bring great blessing to the world.

RISING OPPOSITION

Jesus was very popular with the ordinary people. Great crowds flocked to hear his preaching and to see his miracles. But this made many of the Pharisees and teachers of the Law jealous. They were afraid Jesus would take away their power over the people. They rejected him because his message about God's kingdom went against their teaching about the Law.

The Pharisees believed that people could come into God's kingdom only by keeping his commandments. So, they tried to obey God's law, and followed a set of man-made rules and regulations as well. But Jesus said they were wrong: People come into God's kingdom when they accept God's undeserved love and forgiveness.

This was hard for the proud Pharisees to take. It meant that all their good works were useless. Why, even the worst outcasts and sinners could belong to God's kingdom if Jesus' teachings were true! So the Pharisees wanted to get rid of Jesus. They claimed that it was the devil who gave Jesus power. 'Jesus breaks God's law', they said. 'How can he be God's prophet if he is the friend of sinners?'

BIBLE SEARCH
READ MARK 7:1-23.

How did the Pharisees show that they were hypocrites?

Why were rules and regulations so important to them?

How did Jesus overturn their teaching?

HYPOCRITES AND FALSE TEACHERS

One Sabbath day, Jesus went to the synagogue. A man with a paralysed hand was there. Jesus' enemies watched him closely. Would Jesus heal on the Sabbath day? To work on the Sabbath was against their rules. 'What does God's law tell us to do?' Jesus asked. 'To help people on the Sabbath or to harm them?' The leaders had no answer; but, when Jesus healed the man, they were full of anger and hatred against him.

Jesus spoke out strongly against the Pharisees and teachers of the Law. 'You don't practise what you preach', he told them. 'You make up your **own rules**, and then think God will have to accept you because you keep them. But you end up breaking **God's commandments**. You do your good deeds just to show off how holy you are. You honour God with words, but your heart is far from him. The outcasts who humbly turn to God will come into his kingdom, but you are too proud to enter. You won't go in yourselves, and you stop others from entering. It will be terrible for you, for God will punish you for rejecting me and his kingdom.'

The Pharisees and teachers of the Law were furious with Jesus for calling them false teachers. They had made up their minds about him: God had not sent him; he was a dangerous upstart who had to be destroyed! So they made plans to kill him.

'WHO DO MEN SAY THAT I AM?'

The people who met Jesus or heard of him had to make up their minds about him. They had to answer the question: 'What do you think of Christ? Are you for him or against him?' Many turned away from Jesus when they realized that he would not be an earthly king. They were not interested in the kingdom which Jesus had come to establish. Only a few people were his true followers.

As Jesus travelled with his disciples near the town of Caesarea Philippi, he asked them what people were saying about him. 'Some think you are John the Baptist, or Elijah, or some other great prophet', they replied. Then Jesus asked them directly: 'Who do **you** think I am?' Peter immediately spoke up and said: 'You are the Messiah, the Son of the living God'.

God had led Peter to understand the truth about Jesus. On this great truth God would build his Church. Nothing in heaven or earth could stop God gathering in his chosen people.

At this time, Jesus began to prepare his disciples for the suffering which he knew was ahead of him. But, although he told them plainly that he must die, they did not understand what he was saying.

BIBLE SEARCH
READ MATTHEW 16:13–23.
Why was the truth about Jesus so important?

How could God use Peter?

Why did Jesus get angry with Peter when he said that Jesus should not have to die?

JESUS SHOWS HIS GLORY

One day, Jesus led three of his disciples, Peter, James and John, up on to a high mountain for a time of prayer. As Jesus was praying, an amazing change came over him. His face began to shine like the sun, and his clothes became dazzling white. Suddenly, Moses and Elijah appeared, talking to Jesus about the suffering which would soon come on him. Then a shining cloud came over them, and a voice spoke from the cloud: 'This is my own dear Son with whom I am pleased. Listen to him!'

The disciples were so terrified by what was happening that they threw themselves face down on the ground. But Jesus came and touched them. 'Don't be afraid', he told them. When they looked up, only Jesus was there with them once again.

This vision of Jesus revealed his glory as the Son of God. But the time was not right for others to hear about it. Therefore, as they came down the mountain, Jesus commanded his disciples not to tell what they had seen.

It was now time for Jesus to go to Jerusalem for the Passover. He knew that his enemies there wanted to kill him. But he had come to fulfil his Father's plan. So, he set out for the Holy City, where he would give up his life for the sins of the world.

BIBLE SEARCH
READ MATTHEW 17:1–9.
This vision of Jesus is called his 'transfiguration'.

Why did Jesus let a few of his disciples see his glory?

How did his transfiguration point back to his baptism?

Why did Jesus not want the three disciples to tell what they had seen?

THE MAIN POINTS

- As Jesus carried on his work, people had to make up their minds whether they were for him or against him.

  Some rejected him, and despised his teaching. Leaders among the Jews came to hate him and to plot his death.

  Some believed in Jesus, and accepted him as the Messiah. Peter spoke for all believers when confessing his faith that Jesus was the Son of God.

- It was according to God's plan that Jesus should be hated and rejected. Through the suffering of his Son, God would save the world from sin, death, and the power of Satan.

- To prepare for his suffering, Jesus was transfigured before three of his disciples to show them his glory.

KEY BIBLE PASSAGE   JOHN 6:66–69

Through Jesus we can come to the Father and have eternal life.
Why did some people reject Jesus' teaching?
How does the word of Jesus bring eternal life?

FOR US TODAY

1. 'What do you think of Christ?' is still the most important question for people today. God's people confess their faith that Jesus is their Lord and Saviour.

   Read Romans 10:9–13.
   > Why do believers confess their faith in Jesus?
   > How can you let other people know that you believe in Jesus?

2. A group of boys were talking together during recess. One of them started to make fun of Jim because he went to church and Sunday-school. Harry spoke up for him, saying that being a Christian was nothing to be ashamed of. Some rubbished Harry for doing this.
   > Why did it take courage for Harry to speak up?
   > How could his confession of Christ help others?

WORSHIP

Heavenly Father, thank you for sending your Son to be our Saviour. Give us a firm faith in him, and help us to confess him as our Lord and Saviour by word and deed. Amen.

WITH YOUR FAMILY

Through your congregation, obtain some tracts which tell of Jesus the Saviour. Get your family to help you to distribute these tracts in letterboxes or by handing them to people.

As a devotion, read Matthew 16:13–19 and discuss the meaning of the Second Article of the Creed. Use the hymn 'Fairest Lord Jesus' as a closing prayer.

MORE CHALLENGES

1. John's Gospel records long discussions between Jesus and the Jewish leaders and people. Read one of these discussions in John 7:25–52. What questions were the people asking? How did Jesus answer them?

2. Read how Jesus drove the money-changers out of the temple in Matthew 21:12–16. Why was Jesus so angry? What made the Jewish leaders angry? How did Jesus reply?

3. Study the words of the Apostles' and Nicene Creeds, and see what they confess about Jesus. Sum this up in your own words. Share your creed with the class.

4. Discuss whether your class could undertake a survey in your school asking what people think about Christ.

5. Read Luke 11:37–53. Discuss why Jesus spoke out so strongly against the Pharisees.

Scripture references: Matthew 16:13–23; 17:1–9; Mark 3:1–6; 7:1–23.

Holy week

Holy Week is one of the most sacred times of the year for Christians. During this week, the church prepares for the most important festivals of the church-year.

What is meant by 'Holy Week'?
Why is it called this?
When does it begin? When does it end?

The time for Jesus' final suffering had come. On Palm Sunday, Jesus was welcomed into Jerusalem with glad shouts as the Messiah, the Son of David. Yet, before the week was over, he was mocked and rejected, and finally put to death as a common criminal. Jesus entered the Holy City to die — to offer his life as a perfect sacrifice for the sins of the world.

HAIL TO THE SON OF DAVID

Jesus and his disciples were heading for Jerusalem to celebrate the Passover. The city was already crowded with thousands of pilgrims. Down the slopes of the Mount of Olives Jesus came toward the city gate, riding on a donkey. The crowd travelling with Jesus began to shout: 'Praise to David's Son. God bless the coming kingdom of David our father.' Filled with excitement, they laid their coats on the ground and waved palm branches to welcome Jesus as their king. People coming out of the city joined in the enthusiastic welcome. As Jesus rode through the gates, the whole city was buzzing with excitement.

THE BETRAYAL

When the leaders of the Jews saw how the people hailed Jesus as their king, they were filled with anger and jealousy. The Sadducees (the chief priests and rulers among the Jews) joined with the Pharisees to plan Jesus' death. 'This man is becoming more and more dangerous', they said to one another. 'We must get rid of him!'

In the following days, their hatred of Jesus increased. Again and again they tried to trap him with questions, and attacked his teaching. They looked for a chance to capture him. But this would have to be done secretly, so that the common people would not get upset.

Judas Iscariot, one of Jesus' disciples, gave them their chance. He was the treasurer of Jesus' band, and a thief who stole from their funds. Judas let Satan take control of his heart and turn him against Jesus.

BIBLE SEARCH
READ MATTHEW 21:1-11.

What Old Testament prophecy did Jesus fulfil by riding into Jerusalem as king?

Why did the people welcome him so enthusiastically?

What made their welcome misguided and hollow?

Going secretly to the Jewish leaders, Judas promised to betray his master for 30 silver coins. He would lead them to Jesus in a quiet spot away from the crowd. Now the leaders waited for the right time to arrest Jesus.

BIBLE SEARCH
READ MATTHEW 21:33–46.

What did Jesus mean by this parable?
Why did the leaders want to get rid of Jesus?

THE LAST TIMES

Jesus loved the city of Jerusalem. Looking down on it from the Mount of Olives, he felt sad as he thought how many of the Jews had rejected him. 'God will punish this city once again', he told his disciples. 'Jerusalem will be completely destroyed, and its people will suffer terribly.'

Jesus told his disciples what they should expect to happen in the times until the end. 'There will be great trouble throughout the world: wars, famines, earthquakes, and disasters. False teachers will come, and many people will be deceived. You will be persecuted as you go out into the world telling people about me and the Kingdom. When the Gospel has been preached throughout the world for a witness to me, the end will come.'

Jesus also told them that he would return in glory to judge all people. Those who love and trust in him will then enter everlasting life; but those who do not believe in him will be sent to everlasting punishment. 'Be prepared', he warned his followers. 'You don't know the day or the hour when the Son of Man will come.'

THE LORD'S SUPPER

Jesus knew that soon he would be arrested and put to death. He wanted to share a last meal with his disciples. So he gathered them together on Thursday evening to celebrate the Passover feast in the upper room of a house in Jerusalem.

There were many things Jesus wanted to talk about before he left them. Knowing of Judas' evil plans, he suddenly said: 'One of you is going to betray me!' The disciples were shocked and wondered who it would be. When Judas realized that Jesus knew what he was going to do, he quickly left the room. He made up his mind to help the Jewish rulers capture Jesus that very evening.

As they were eating the Passover, Jesus took some bread, gave thanks, and handed it to his disciples. 'This is my body which is given for you', he told them. Then he took a cup of wine, gave thanks, and gave it to them to drink, saying, 'This is my blood of the new testament, shed for you for the forgiveness of your sins'.

Jesus told his disciples to celebrate this feast of the new covenant in memory of him and his death. Through this sacred meal, God's people would give thanks to him for his gift of the Saviour and for making them his own.

THE HOUR HAS COME

After Jesus had finished speaking and praying with his disciples, he took the disciples with him to a quiet garden on the side of the Mount of Olives. The hour of his great suffering had come. In a strange and mysterious way, God would save the world through the sacrifice of his own Son.

BIBLE SEARCH
READ MATTHEW 26:26–28.

Why did Jesus give the Lord's Supper?

Discuss why he gave the Lord's Supper as he celebrated the Passover feast with his disciples.

Why do God's people especially treasure this sacred meal?

WHAT THE LESSON TEACHES US

- God's great plan was reaching its climax. Jesus was welcomed into Jerusalem as the Messiah, the Son of David.

- Jesus came as king to suffer and to die as a sacrifice for the sins of the world. God would establish his everlasting kingdom through the death of his Son.

- Jesus gave the Lord's Supper as the Sacrament of his body and blood. Through this sacred meal, God's people receive his love and forgiveness, and proclaim the Good News of the kingdom.

KEY BIBLE PASSAGE **JOHN 18:33–37**

Jesus came as king, but his kingdom is 'not of this world'. Only those who understand and believe the truth about Jesus enter God's kingdom.

What is Jesus' kingdom?
How do people enter it?

GOD'S PEOPLE TODAY

1. Jesus is the Christ. God's people today believe and confess this. They honour and serve Jesus as their king.

   Read 1 John 5:1–5.
   How can we show that Jesus is our king?

2. People often make fun of those who follow Jesus as their king. Sometimes they even persecute them.

   Why do so many people reject Jesus as Lord?
   Why do they sometimes persecute his followers?
   How should we act if people make fun of us for being Christians?

WORSHIP

Fairest Lord Jesus, King of creation,
Son of God, and Son of Man,
Glory and honour, praise, adoration,
Ever be thine, and thine alone.

Lord Jesus, help us always to honour you as our king, and to live for your praise and glory. Amen.

Bible references: Matthew 21:1 – 26:35; Mark 11:1 – 14:31; Luke 19:28 – 22:38; John 13:1 – 17:26.

THE FOLK AT HOME

Get your family to help you make this poster and display it in your home.

As a devotion, read the story of Jesus' entry into Jerusalem as king: Luke 19:28–40. Members of the family could suggest what it means that Christ is king. Close with a prayer, thanking Jesus for coming to be our king and for being willing to suffer for us.

MORE TO DO

1. Talk about some of the things Jesus did on the days of Holy Week leading up to Good Friday. You could set out some of the main events on a chart.

2. Read how Jesus washed his disciples' feet: John 13:1–10. Discuss why Jesus did this, and what we can learn from it.

3. Why did Jesus feel so sad about Jerusalem? Read Matthew 23:37 – 24:14; 24:29–31, and discuss the signs Jesus tells us to expect. Why has Jesus not yet returned for judgment?

4. Choose one of the parables Jesus told in Matthew 25, and discuss what it teaches us today. You could prepare it in the form of a skit for use in the class.

5. After a Holy Communion service, ask some of the older members of the congregation what the Sacrament means to them.

26

The day Jesus died

The Good Friday service was about to begin. Paraments on the altar and pulpit were black; there were no flowers in the sanctuary, and the wall banners had been taken down. As the people sang the first hymn, a rough wooden cross was carried in procession through the congregation and placed beside the altar . . . The people of God had gathered to commemorate the day that Jesus died.

Why is this day called 'Good Friday'?
Why is it such a holy day for Christians?

'Guilty! All people are sinful and deserve my punishment.' That was God's judgment on the human race.

But God is love. He does not want anyone to perish; he wants all people to live with him for ever in perfect happiness. So, gradually down through the centuries, he had unfolded his great plan to save mankind from sin and punishment. And now the time had come for him to carry out the crucial part of his plan.

JESUS IN GETHSEMANE

As Jesus approached the Garden of Gethsemane with his disciples, he became very sad and distressed. He knew that he had to take on himself the sins of the whole world and to bear their punishment. He knew that he had to die.

There, in the quiet of the garden, Jesus prayed earnestly to his Father, asking him to take away this terrible suffering if it were possible. 'But not my will be done. Your will must be done', he prayed. To save the world, Jesus **had to suffer and die**; that **was** his Father's will and his Father's plan. So, after a time of struggle and agony, Jesus prepared to go to his death.

BIBLE SEARCH
READ MATTHEW 26:36–46.
Discuss Jesus' prayer, and why he was in such agony.

ARRESTED

After praying by himself for the third time, Jesus went back and woke up his disciples. At that very moment, a large band of men with burning torches was coming near. Judas was leading the soldiers and servants of the high priest who had come to arrest Jesus.

Judas went straight up to Jesus and kissed him on the cheek. Now the soldiers knew whom to seize. Peter wanted to fight. He struck at one of the men with his sword, cutting off his ear. But Jesus immediately stopped him. He told Peter to put away his sword, and healed the man's ear. The disciples, terrified at what was happening, all fled, leaving Jesus alone with his enemies.

The soldiers tied Jesus up and took him back into the city to be tried by Caiaphas, the high priest. During the night, Jesus was treated cruelly by his enemies. He was brought before the Jewish Council and falsely accused of evil-doing. He was mocked and beaten by the men who were guarding him. When daylight came, Jesus was brought before the Council once again, and condemned to death falsely for claiming to be God's Son.

BIBLE SEARCH
READ LUKE 22:54–62.

Why did Peter deny Jesus?
How did Jesus help him even then?

SUFFERED UNDER PONTIUS PILATE

The Jewish leaders did not have authority to put anyone to death; only the Roman Governor could do this. So Jesus was led to Pontius Pilate to be sentenced. Pilate soon realized that Jesus had done nothing wrong. He knew of the jealousy of the Jewish leaders, and wanted to set Jesus free. But the high priests stirred up the crowd to shout for Jesus to be crucified. Afraid of a riot, Pilate weakly gave in to them, and commanded that Jesus be whipped, and then crucified.

CRUCIFIED

At about 9 o'clock in the morning, the Roman soldiers led Jesus out to be crucified with two other criminals. As Jesus carried part of the cross on his bleeding shoulders, he collapsed. When he could carry it no further, the soldiers forced a man called Simon to carry it for him.

The sad procession went out through the city gates to a hill shaped like a skull. There, at Calvary, the soldiers nailed Jesus to his cross, and erected it between crosses bearing two thieves. 'Father, forgive them', Jesus cried. 'They don't know what they are doing!'

DEAD

As Jesus hung on the cross in great pain, his enemies made fun of him. Mockingly, they cried: 'If you are the Son of God, come down from the cross. He saved others, but he can't save himself!' Then, at about 12 midday, a strange darkness came over the land. People watching grew afraid and slunk away in the gloom.

Jesus experienced great agony of body and soul as his Father laid on him the guilt and punishment for the sins of the world. In his deep suffering he cried out: 'My God, my God, why have you forsaken me?' Then, at about 3 o'clock, he called out loudly: 'It is finished. Father, into your hands I place my spirit.' After this, he bowed his head and died.

Some time later, the soldiers came and pierced Jesus' side with a spear, to make sure he was dead.

As Jesus died, the ground shook and the curtain in the temple was split in two. When the army officer in charge of the crucifixion saw the earthquake and how Jesus died, he cried out: 'He really was the Son of God!'

BIBLE SEARCH

Read one of the Gospel accounts of how Jesus died, and share your feelings about it:

MATTHEW 27:32-45.　　**MARK 15:21-39.**
LUKE 23:26-47.　　　　**JOHN 19:16-37.**

BURIED

Before 6 o'clock that evening, Jesus' body was taken down from the cross by his friends. A rich man named Joseph of Arimathea got permission to bury Jesus in his own garden nearby. These friends wrapped Jesus' body in linen cloth with spices, and laid him in a new tomb cut out of the rock. Then a large stone was rolled in front of the tomb.

Jesus' enemies wanted to make sure that no one would take away his body. Pilate gave the Jewish leaders permission to place a special guard on the tomb, and a seal was placed on the stone.

Jesus lay dead in the grave. It seemed as though his enemies had destroyed him, as though all the hopes of his disciples had come to nothing. But this was according to God's plan. His Son would yet win the victory!

ACCORDING TO PLAN

- In his great love, God himself saved the world from sin. He carried out his plan of salvation through the suffering and death of his own dear Son.

- Jesus **bore the sins of all people**, so that they could be forgiven and be put right with God.

- Jesus **bore the anger and punishment of God** which people deserved, so that they could receive God's love.

- Jesus **died**, to conquer death and bring hope of everlasting life.

ALL THIS WAS ACCORDING TO PLAN — GOD'S PLAN.

KEY BIBLE PASSAGE　　**1 PETER 1:18-20**

The Jews sacrificed a special lamb at the Passover feast to remember how God had saved them from slavery in Egypt. God's Son died as the Lamb of God to set all people free from sin and death for ever.

Why did God lay the sin of the world on his own Son?
How could the sacrifice of Jesus take away sin?

GOD'S PEOPLE TODAY

1. Saved! Set free from sin! That's the Good News for **us**.

   'At great cost Jesus has saved and redeemed me, a lost and condemned person. He has freed me from sin, death, and the power of the devil, not with silver or gold, but with his holy and precious blood and his innocent suffering and death.' (Martin Luther)

   Read 2 Corinthians 5:21.
      Tell what it means to you that Jesus died for you.

2. We are saved — to serve. Martin Luther puts it this way:

   'All this he has done that I may be his own, live under him in his kingdom, and serve him in everlasting righteousness, innocence, and blessedness.'
      Why should we live for God?
      How can we live for God?

WORSHIP

Thank you, Lord Jesus, for giving your life for us to save us from sin, death, and the power of the devil. Help us to live as your people and to serve you as long as we live. In your name we pray. Amen.

Bible references: Matthew 26:36–75; 27; Mark 14:32–72; 15; Luke 22:39–71; 23; John 18; 19.

WITH YOUR FAMILY

Get your family to help you draw a picture of Good Friday to display in your home.

For a devotion, read 1 Peter 1:18–20, and the words of Luther in the left column. Close your devotion with the hymn 'When I survey the wondrous cross'.

THANK YOU JESUS

MORE TO DO

1. Study the various trials of Jesus and discuss how he was treated: John 18:12,13,19–23; Mark 14:53, 55–65; 15:1; Luke 23:1–24; Matthew 27:27–31.

2. Name your favourite hymns telling of Jesus' death as our Saviour, and sing them in class.

3. Jesus spoke seven times as he was dying on the cross. Find out what he said, and discuss these sayings: Luke 23:34; 23:43; John 19:26,27; Matthew 27:46; John 19:28; 19:30; Luke 23:46.

4. Decide on some practical way that you, as a class, could show your thankfulness to Jesus.

5. Read what happened to Judas in Matthew 27:3–8. Discuss the sad story of this man.

27

Jesus wins the victory

The key-stone is most important in the plans for building an arch; the whole arch depends on it. Remove that stone, and the whole arch collapses. But with the key-stone securely in place, the arch stands firm.

Easter Sunday is like the key-stone in God's plans. Jesus had died as the sin-bearer. If he had remained dead, then sin would have won — because the wages of sin is death.

But on Easter Sunday God had a marvellous victory. In great power and majesty, Jesus rose from the dead. He had destroyed sin and death. He had overcome the power of Satan.

God's whole plan was built around this key-stone: 'Jesus is alive! He has won the victory. Christ is Lord, to the glory of God the Father.' God will accomplish all that he planned to do.

God chose certain people to be witnesses of the resurrection of Jesus. In the four Gospels they tell us the story of how Jesus rose.
The following accounts are what some of those involved on Easter Sunday might have told their friends.

THE ACCOUNT OF THE GUARDS

All was peaceful as we stood guard at the tomb on that Sunday morning. Then, suddenly, the ground shook under us. A bright, shining being appeared, and rolled away the stone from the front of the tomb. The grave was empty! We were terrified, and ran to tell the Jewish leaders. They paid us not to report what had happened, but to say that Jesus' disciples had stolen the body during the night. We have spread this tale. Some seem to believe it, but we know it is a lie!

THE ACCOUNT OF MARY, MOTHER OF JAMES

We went to the tomb just as the sun was rising on Sunday morning. We wanted to finish anointing Jesus. Suddenly we remembered the large stone. Who would roll it away for us? But as we came close, we saw that the stone had already been rolled away!

Mary Magdalene immediately thought that someone had stolen Jesus' body, and ran to tell Peter and John. But we went on into the tomb — and got a great shock. An angel, whose face shone like lightning, was in the tomb.

'Don't be afraid', he told us. 'Jesus is alive! He has been raised from the dead. See, his body is no longer here. Now, go and tell his disciples that he is alive, and that he will meet them in Galilee.'

CONT . . .

We could hardly believe our ears — yet it was true. We were glad — yet scared, too! We ran to tell the others what had happened . . . Suddenly Jesus himself stood in front of us. 'Peace be with you', he said. We fell down and worshipped him. We actually held his feet. It was Jesus — alive again. Then he was gone, and we rushed to tell the disciples . . .

THE ACCOUNT OF PETER AND JOHN

Mary arrived, all upset, to tell us someone must have stolen Jesus' body. We both ran as fast as we could to see what had happened. Jesus' body was not there! But it didn't look as though it had been stolen. The grave clothes were lying neatly in place, undisturbed.

When we returned to the house, the other women came to tell us their amazing news: 'Jesus is risen!' But it just seemed impossible . . .

THE ACCOUNT OF MARY MAGDALENE

I went back to the tomb after Peter and John had left, and stood there crying.

I noticed a man standing behind me, and thought it was the gardener. 'Please help me find Jesus' body', I begged him. 'Mary!' he said, and suddenly I recognized him. It was Jesus — alive again! I felt like clinging to him so that he would never go away again. But he told me not to hold on to him. 'Share the good news with my disciples', he said. 'Tell them that I will soon be returning to my heavenly Father.' Well, I did tell them, but a lot of them wouldn't believe me . . .

THE ACCOUNT OF CLEOPAS

We were rather confused about the news of the women as we walked back to Emmaus. As we were chatting, a stranger began to walk along with us. As we talked about the sad events of the past days and the strange news of the women, he started explaining the Old Testament Scriptures to us. He showed us clearly from what the prophets had said that the Messiah had to die and rise again.

When we arrived in Emmaus, we asked the stranger to have the evening meal with us. As he said grace, our eyes were suddenly opened. It was **Jesus** — alive again! But then he disappeared from our sight. So we just had to share the good news, so we ran as fast as we could back to Jerusalem to tell the others . . .

BIBLE SEARCH
READ LUKE 24:36–45.

Why were the disciples so frightened?

How did Jesus prove that he had risen?

Why can **we** be sure he is risen?

THE ACCOUNT OF THOMAS

I was not there that Sunday evening, but the others told me the stunning news that Jesus had appeared alive again. It seemed quite impossible to me! I vowed that I wasn't going to believe it unless I could actually touch the nail scars and the spear-wound in his side. A week later, I was with the others in the upper room, and suddenly Jesus stood in front of me. He showed me his hands and feet. It was true! He was alive! Even death could not beat him. He is God! He is my Lord!

BIBLE SEARCH
READ JOHN 21:1–14.

Why did Peter and the others return to Galilee?
Why was Peter sure it was Jesus on the shore?
Discuss what is special about this appearance of the living Lord.

OTHER APPEARANCES

During the next few weeks, Jesus showed himself alive to his disciples again and again. He left them in no doubt that he truly had won the victory over sin and death. He met more than 500 of his followers on a mountain in Galilee, and convinced them that he was alive. He told them of his plans for them. 'You shall be my witnesses. Go everywhere, telling the good news about forgiveness and salvation. I will be with you always to the end of the age.'

BIBLE SEARCH
READ 1 CORINTHIANS 15:3–8.

Discuss the various appearances of Jesus referred to by Paul. List other times Jesus showed himself alive to his followers.

THE SURE FOUNDATION

- All that God planned will happen! The resurrection of Jesus makes this completely certain.

- Jesus is the Son of God. His resurrection revealed his glory, and showed that he has power over all things.

- Jesus has overcome sin and conquered death. His resurrection makes it certain that our sins are forgiven, and that we, too, shall rise from the dead.

- God revealed the truth about Jesus' victory to chosen witnesses. We can trust what they tell us.

KEY BIBLE PASSAGE   **1 CORINTHIANS 15:17–20**

God's plan centres on the resurrection of Jesus. His victory is the guarantee of our salvation.
Why does the forgiveness of sins depend on Jesus' resurrection?
How does it guarantee our resurrection?

GOD'S PEOPLE TODAY

1. On Easter Sunday, Christians celebrate Jesus' victory. It is a joyful day for us. Jesus is alive! He is with us.

    How do we celebrate on Easter Sunday?

    Read 1 Corinthians 15:55–57.

    Why is Paul so joyful and confident? Should we be afraid of dying?

2. Knowing that Jesus is alive helps us in our daily life. How could this help us:

    ...if we were put in jail because of our faith?

    ...if we became seriously ill and thought we might die?

    ...if we have doubts about God?

WORSHIP

Celebrate Jesus' victory by singing a favourite Easter hymn.

LITANY PRAYER:

The Lord is risen:
The Lord is risen indeed.
For your great victory:
We thank and praise you, Jesus.
For your great power and glory:
We thank and praise you, Jesus.
That we may gladly follow you as Lord:
Grant us, dear Lord. Amen.

WITH THE FAMILY

Make an Easter mobile which shows our joy at Jesus' resurrection. Hang the mobile near the table where you eat together.

As a devotion, read John 21:1–14. Members of the family could share what it means to them that Jesus is their risen Lord. Sing (or read) the Easter hymn 'I know that my Redeemer lives'.

MORE CHALLENGES

1. Read one of the Gospel accounts of Jesus' rising from the dead, e.g., John 20:1–23. Imagine you are one of the eye-witnesses. Share how you feel. Discuss how your life will change because of this experience.

2. On posters around the classroom, write short sentences of praise to Jesus, the victor over sin and death.

3. Read Romans 6:1–4. How does your baptism make you share in Good Friday and Easter Sunday? Write a prayer, telling how you feel about Jesus' dying and rising again, and about your own baptism.

4. Discuss various Christian Easter customs, and talk about Easter symbols.

Scripture references: Matthew 28; Mark 16; Luke 24; John 20,21.

Power from on high

In 1861, Pastor Nommensen began work as a Christian missionary among the Batak people in North Sumatra. He came face to face with the power of evil spirits among these people. Enemies violently opposed his teaching and tried to kill him. But God protected him and gave him courage as he kept on telling the people about Jesus. The power of the Gospel turned more and more people away from Satan's rule and led them to accept Jesus as their Lord. By 1918, when Pastor Nommensen died, 180,000 people had been baptized as Christians.

What power was at work through Pastor Nommensen? What power opposed this work? Why did many Bataks become Christians?

On the firm foundation of Jesus' resurrection, God planned to build his Church. His plan included using Jesus' followers to carry out the challenging task of gathering in his New Testament people.

But the disciples of Jesus were weak and imperfect. How could God carry out such a great plan through them? God himself came, to give these followers of Jesus special power, so that they would go out everywhere, boldly telling the Good News of the kingdom of God. In this way God put the new stage of his plan into operation.

ASCENDED INTO HEAVEN

Forty days after Easter Sunday, Jesus met with his disciples for the final time, and told them that he was going back to his Father. 'You will be my witnesses. Beginning in Jerusalem, you will go out to the ends of the earth, telling the Good News of forgiveness in my name. But now, wait for the Holy Spirit to come upon you. He will teach and strengthen you so that you can be my missionaries.'

Jesus led his apostles out of Jerusalem to the little town called Bethany. He raised his hands to bless them. As they watched, he was taken up from them until a cloud covered him from sight. He ascended into heaven to be crowned with honour and glory. Now he is ruling over all things at God's right hand. All authority as Lord and King is his in heaven and earth.

BIBLE SEARCH
READ ACTS 1:1–5.

Why did Jesus keep on appearing to his disciples for forty days?

Why were Jesus' disciples now called 'apostles'?

119

As the apostles stood looking up, two angels suddenly appeared. They asked them why they were looking up into the sky. 'Jesus will come back in the same way you saw him go to heaven', they said.

So the apostles returned to Jerusalem to wait for Jesus to keep his promise to send them special help and power. While they waited, they gathered with other believers to pray and to worship Jesus. So that there still would be 12 apostles, they chose Matthias to take the place of Judas, who had killed himself.

Suddenly, the house was filled with a great noise, like the sound of a mighty wind. What looked like tongues of fire spread out and rested on the disciples. They were filled with great joy, and began to speak in many languages, telling the wonderful things that God had done.

The Holy Spirit had come on them to give them power. Now they could more fully understand God's plan and all that he had done through Jesus. They felt quite unafraid, and wanted to tell the good news that all could be forgiven and become God's people because of Christ, the Saviour.

 ## PENTECOST DAY

Fifty days after Easter, the Jews in Jerusalem celebrated another special festival. This was a feast of thanksgiving called Pentecost. Jerusalem was filled with people from many different countries. The apostles, together with about 120 other followers of Jesus, had come together in the upper room to pray.

BIBLE SEARCH
READ ACTS 2:5–13.

Why did the Holy Spirit come on Pentecost Day?

Why did the believers speak to people in their own languages?

What did this show about God's plans for his New Testament Church?

GOOD NEWS FOR ALL PEOPLE

People in Jerusalem heard the loud noise and came to investigate. Many of them were visitors who spoke different languages. The believers walked among them telling, in these various languages, the great things God had done. This amazed the people who realized that the believers were all Galileans. But some scoffed, saying that they were just drunk.

Peter stood up, and with a loud voice began to preach to the crowd. He was not afraid now. Boldly he explained what was happening. God had kept his promise, and had sent them his Holy Spirit. Then he told the people of God's great plan by which he sent his own Son to be the Messiah. 'You killed Jesus by letting sinful men crucify him', Peter said, 'yet even this was according to God's plan. God has raised Jesus from the dead, and he is now ruling as King at God's right hand.'

Peter's preaching made a great impression on the people. 'What should we do?' they asked. Peter replied: 'Repent of your sins and be baptized in Jesus' name, so that you may be forgiven and become God's people'.

The Holy Spirit worked powerfully through the Word which Peter and the other apostles preached. About 3,000 people believed the message and were baptized. As new followers of Jesus, they gladly came together in fellowship day by day to hear the apostles' teaching and to pray. So, the first Christian congregation was formed.

The new stage of God's great plan had begun. Through the power of the Holy Spirit, people would be gathered in from all countries to be the Church of Jesus Christ, the new Israel of God.

BIBLE SEARCH
READ ACTS 2:14–37.

How had Peter changed since Good Friday?

How did Peter show that Jesus was truly the Messiah?

What effect did his preaching have?

THESE ARE THE HEADLINES

- Forty days after Easter, Jesus ascended into heaven. God exalted him to rule over all things in heaven and on earth.

- On Pentecost Day, the Holy Spirit came on the disciples of Jesus to give them power to be his witnesses.

- Through the preaching of the Gospel and Baptism, the Holy Spirit led thousands of people to believe in Jesus as their Saviour and Lord.

- All who believed in Jesus were gathered into the new community of the holy Christian Church, the people of God of the new covenant.

KEY BIBLE PASSAGE **ACTS 2:38,39**

The Holy Spirit came with God's power to bring people to faith and to make them the people of God.

What does God promise to those who repent and are baptized?

Whom does God receive as his people?

How does the Holy Spirit build the Church of God?

GOD'S PEOPLE TODAY

1. God has made us his people today, by his grace, through the power of the Holy Spirit.

   Read Titus 3:4,5.
   > How does the Holy Spirit come on us with his power?
   > What are the results of the Spirit's work in us?

2. Discuss why we need the Holy Spirit, and how he can help the following people:
   > Harry doubts whether there is a God.
   >
   > Mr & Mrs Lucas are planning to have their baby baptized soon.
   >
   > Jenny is scared to tell her friends that she is a Christian.
   >
   > Mary wants to lead her best friend to Christ.

WORSHIP

Dear God, we know that by our own understanding or effort we cannot believe in Jesus Christ or come to him. We thank you for giving us your Holy Spirit, who has brought us to faith. Give us power to live as those who belong to you, and to tell others the good news of Jesus our Saviour. In his name we pray. Amen.

Scripture references: Luke 24:50–52; Acts 1; 2:1–42.

THE FOLK AT HOME

Work out a simple quiz on the Bible stories about Jesus' ascension and Pentecost Day. Get the members of your family to answer it.

As a family devotion, read the story of Pentecost as told in this chapter, and discuss the questions listed under Bible Search: Acts 2:5–13. Close the devotion with a Pentecost hymn.

MORE CHALLENGES

1. Who is the Holy Spirit? Read 1 Corinthians 2:10–12 and discuss the Bible teaching about him. What symbols are used to represent him? Why have these symbols been chosen?

2. Jesus ascended into heaven to sit at God's right hand. Discuss what this means.

3. Compare the story of Pentecost Day with the Tower of Babel (Genesis 11:1–9). Discuss God's plan to unite all people once again through his Church.

4. Write the story of Jesus' ascension or of Pentecost Day as though you were a newspaper journalist. Share what you have written with the class.

5. Make this banner or poster as a class project. Display it in church.

29

God's Spirit at work

It was a happy occasion for the St Paul's congregation. At the Sunday service, nine people became members of the congregation, three of them through Holy Baptism. 'Welcome to the family', the pastor said at the luncheon after the service, assuring them of the loving support of the congregation. The new members enjoyed the fellowship and the warm welcome of the people. They felt that they had become part of a big, loving family.

What is a Christian congregation?
How is the Holy Spirit at work in a congregation?

By his coming with special power, the Holy Spirit created the first Christian congregation in Jerusalem. He kept on working in this new community of believers. He made their faith in Jesus stronger, and helped them to love one another. He also gave them the power to witness for Jesus. Through this congregation, God began his plan to spread the good news of salvation to the far corners of the earth.

A FELLOWSHIP OF LOVE

What happened in that first congregation? What was the life of the people like? In these imaginary letters, Ruth tells her friend Lois, in Antioch in Syria, about the Jerusalem congregation and the events that followed Pentecost Day.

Jerusalem

Dear Lois,

Greetings in Jesus' name. I hope you had a safe journey back to Antioch after Pentecost. Wonderful things have been happening here since then. All of us who follow Jesus are a big, happy family. Every day we meet in Solomon's Porch in the temple to worship and to hear the teaching of the apostles. You can feel the love and friendliness among the people. We also share meals in each other's homes, and praise God together for his love.

As you know, our family never had much money. Well, we don't go short of anything now. Our fellow-believers keep sharing their goods with us and others who are poor. Peter keeps on reminding us that one of the best ways we can show Jesus' love is by helping other people. Nowadays we often invite our neighbours to our place and tell them about Jesus. Every day more and more people are joining us. Praise God that the Holy Spirit is working so powerfully in Jerusalem . . .

Your loving friend,

Ruth

123

Dear Lois,
Jerusalem

God be with you. I hope your family is well. The Holy Spirit is doing wonderful miracles through the apostles. The other day Peter and John healed a man who had been unable to walk for many years. It was incredible! At Peter's command in Jesus' name, the man just got up from his couch and started jumping around and praising God. Peter told the crowd which gathered how Jesus had done this miracle through them. I heard him explain how God's promise to bless all the people on earth was coming true through Jesus. Then he called on them to repent and to enter God's kingdom as believers in Jesus, his Son.

But we are worried about the Jewish leaders. They hate all of us! They dragged Peter and John before the Council, and commanded them to stop preaching about Jesus. But Peter was not scared of them, praise God! He said he would keep right on preaching because God wanted him to. How can any of us stop talking about Jesus? There is no other Saviour!

More and more miracles are being done by the apostles, and many people are joining us day by day. There are about 5,000 believers now. But I'm sure there's going to be trouble. The leaders hate all this, and will try to stop it. Pray for us, Lois!

Your loving friend,

Ruth

BIBLE SEARCH
READ ACTS 4:32–37.

Talk about the first Christian congregation and the life of the people.

Why was the witness of these early Christians so effective?

Jerusalem

Dear Lois,

What I was scared of has happened! Stephen was stoned to death today. He was one of the seven helpers chosen to assist the apostles in their work. Stephen had a really strong faith in Jesus. But his bold witness for Jesus made many enemies for him. Today the Jewish leaders grabbed him and brought him before the Council. They told terrible lies about him. He spoke out boldly, telling them that God had always planned to send the Messiah through Abraham's family, but now they were being stubborn and unbelieving just like their fathers. The leaders couldn't stand the truth. In a furious rage they dragged him out of the city and stoned him. A young man called Saul kept egging them on to kill him. God's ways are strange! Stephen was a wonderful, loving man. Even as he died, he asked God to forgive his enemies.

My husband, Benjamin, is sure that we all face persecution. Well, Jesus warned us of this. One thing I know: We will never give up our faith in him. He is our Lord, for ever.

Greetings,

Ruth

BIBLE SEARCH
READ ACTS 5:17–42.

Why did the apostles speak out so boldly for Jesus?

Discuss Gamaliel's advice to the Council.

124

Dear Lois,
The peace of Jesus be with you! We have to flee from Jerusalem   Jerusalem. Bitter enemies like Saul of Tarsus have begun to throw Jesus' followers into jail and to treat them cruelly. Yet they are giving a strong witness to Jesus even as they suffer. Many of our friends have fled already. Strange! Perhaps, through all this trouble, the Good News about Jesus will be spread everywhere. Benjamin plans to leave secretly as soon as possible. We will come up to you in Antioch.
I must tell you some other news. We have heard that Samaritans, too, have turned to Christ. This surprises us because they are not of our nation, the Jews. But Philip and the apostles have preached the Gospel in their towns, and many have been baptized. It makes us glad to see how more and more are becoming Jesus' followers, and not just here in Jerusalem. Hope to see you soon.

Love,
Ruth

BIBLE SEARCH
READ ACTS 7:51 – 8:3.

Why were the Jews so furious with Stephen?

Why is he called a Christian 'martyr'?

How did God use persecution to spread the Gospel?

THE MAIN POINTS

- The Holy Spirit was at work in the first congregation in Jerusalem, uniting all who believed in Christ in the fellowship of God's family.

- By his power, the Spirit helped believers in their weakness and led them to be faithful servants of Jesus. Through their life of love and worship, God showed what it meant to be a follower of Christ.

- More and more people were led into the church through the witness of these first believers. But, when persecution began, many of them had to flee from Jerusalem.

- The followers of Jesus preached the message about him wherever they went. In this way God began his plan to spread his Church.

KEY BIBLE PASSAGE   ACTS 2:42–47

The first Christian congregation was active in worship, love, and witness.

What is meant by 'Christian fellowship'?
How did this life of fellowship show the Holy Spirit at work?
Why did this first congregation keep on growing?

THIS IS FOR US

1. The Holy Spirit is powerfully at work in God's people today, as he blesses them and strengthens them to serve the Lord Jesus.

Read Galatians 5:22–26.

What are the fruits which the Holy Spirit produces in us?
How can God use these gifts for service in his kingdom?

2. Discuss how the Holy Spirit works through people today. Give examples of this from your own congregation.

WORSHIP

Wake us, O Lord, to human need,
To go wherever you would lead.
Awake our senses so that we
More sensitive to needs may be.

Since you've redeemed us from despair,
You've freed us so that we can share;
Our neighbour's problems now we'll bear;
Because you love, we love and care.

Scripture references: Acts 2:42–47; 3–7; 8:1–3.

WITH YOUR FAMILY

Get your family to help you make this poster of the fruits of the Spirit.

As a devotion, read Galatians 5:22–26 and talk about the various fruits the Spirit gives. Close with a prayer asking the Holy Spirit to bless you with his gifts.

LOVE
JOY
PEACE
PATIENCE
KINDNESS
GOODNESS
FAITHFULNESS
GENTLENESS
SELF-CONTROL

MORE TO DO

1. Read how the Gospel began to spread from Jerusalem:
. . . Acts 8:4–17 — the apostles in Samaria;
. . . Acts 8:26–43 — Philip and the Ethiopian;
. . . Acts 10:32–43 — Peter in Lydda and Joppa.

2. Sometimes problems and troubles arose in the first congregation. Read about one sad thing which happened: Acts 5:1–11. Why did this happen? What can it teach us?

3. Invite a leader in the congregation to talk to your class about the work and mission of the church in your community.

4. If any people have recently joined your congregation, plan to speak to them after a service and make them feel welcome. You could especially befriend children or teenagers.

All one in Christ

30

People of all sorts, of different races, colours, and nations in the world, form the one Church of Jesus Christ. Perhaps right in your own congregation, people from many different countries share in the worship and fellowship of God's own family.

Talk about different kinds of people who belong to your congregation.
Why can people of all nations share in the fellowship of God's Church?

'The whole world is your mission field', Jesus had told his disciples. But just what did this mean?

God led his people to understand more fully his plan to unite all nations in Christ. Beginning with Jewish Christians in Jerusalem, he reached out to people of all races to bring them into his one family, the Church. God even chose one person to be his special missionary to the Gentiles.

'CHRISTIANS'

Some of the believers, fleeing from persecution in Jerusalem, went to Antioch in Syria, and soon a congregation was also formed there. This was the place where followers of the Lord Jesus were first called 'Christians'.

Some believers began to tell the Good News about the Saviour to people who were not of the Jewish race. Many of these people also believed, and became followers of Jesus.

But now an important question arose: Must people become Jews to be Christians? The Jews called the people of all other nations 'Gentiles' or 'heathen', and kept quite separate from them. When Gentiles wanted to be a part of the Jewish community and to worship the true God, they had to accept all the Jewish laws, such as circumcision. Was this what Jesus wanted for **his** Church?

FOR GENTILES ALSO

No, people did **not** need to become Jews to be followers of Christ. All who believed — Greeks, Romans, all nations — could be God's own people, no matter what race they belonged to.

In a strange vision, God showed the Apostle Peter that he should not think of Gentiles as being 'unclean'. He then sent Peter to tell the Good News about Jesus to Cornelius, a Roman soldier in Caesarea. The Holy Spirit led Cornelius and his household to believe in Jesus, and to be baptized. Peter was glad when he realized that God had also given the Gentiles the chance to repent and to be his people.

BIBLE SEARCH
READ ACTS 10:9-15.

Why did Peter eat only certain kinds of food?

What was God preparing him for with this vision?

READ ACTS 10:34-48.

Peter's sermon shows us clearly what the apostles preached about Jesus. Talk about what he said.

Why was Peter surprised and glad when the Holy Spirit came on Cornelius?

It was an exciting discovery for the congregation in Jerusalem when they learnt that God's saving plan also included the Gentiles. Now they had another reason for praising God.

AN AFRICAN BECOMES A CHRISTIAN

Philip was one of the helpers chosen to assist the apostles in Samaria. One day, the Holy Spirit told him to travel down to the desert road which led to Egypt. On the road he met an Ethiopian official riding in a chariot. The man was reading from the book of the prophet Isaiah, about the Servant of God who would be ill-treated and put to death like a lamb that is slaughtered. But he did not understand what he was reading. Philip rode along in his chariot with him, explaining what the prophet had written. He told the black man about Jesus, the Lamb of God who had died for the sins of the world. The Holy Spirit led the Ethiopian to believe in Jesus as his Saviour. When they came to some water, Philip baptized him in the name of Jesus. Then the African continued on his way home, glad that God had made him a member of his family.

APOSTLE TO THE GENTILES

Saul of Tarsus hated Jesus and persecuted his followers in Jerusalem. In his amazing grace, God had planned that this man should become his special apostle to the Gentiles.

One day, Saul was on his way to arrest Christians in Damascus when he had a strange experience . . .

1 Suddenly a bright light shone around Saul, and Jesus appeared in his glory. Saul fell to the ground, blinded. 'Why are you persecuting me, Saul?' Jesus asked him.

2 Saul was shocked. Jesus was alive! He was truly the Son of God! For three days Saul sat in blindness, thinking how terribly wrong his life had been.

3 God sent Ananias to Saul. When he laid his hands on him, Saul was able to see again. Then Ananias baptized him, and Saul became a Christian.

4

Saul immediately began to preach about Jesus in the synagogue. The Jews were furious. 'He has betrayed us', they said, and tried to kill him. But Saul escaped and went down to Jerusalem to talk with the apostles. After this, he returned to his home town for some years.

5

As the work for Jesus in Antioch kept on growing, a man called Barnabas asked Saul to come to Antioch and help in the work. (From then on, Saul was called Paul.) God blessed the work of Paul and other leaders so that many became Christians.

6

The Holy Spirit directed the congregation in Antioch to choose Paul and Barnabas to be his missionaries to the Gentiles. After a special service, Paul and Barnabas set out on their first journey to preach the Gospel in the Gentile world.

 BIBLE SEARCH
READ ACTS 9:1–19.

How was God especially gracious to Saul? Talk about the complete change which came over Saul.

READ ACTS 26:10–18.
Why was Paul so important in God's plans?

In the years which followed, Paul travelled far and wide preaching the Gospel. People from many different races joined the Church of Jesus Christ.

GETTING THE MESSAGE

- A worldwide Church with no barriers between the races: This was God's secret plan for his New Testament people, which he now revealed through the apostles.

- God sent out Paul and other helpers to spread the Gospel throughout the Gentile world. The Church of Jesus Christ would spread to the far corners of the earth.

 **KEY BIBLE PASSAGE**   **EPHESIANS 2:11–14**

Jews and Gentiles are all one in Christ. Through Jesus the Saviour, all believers are united in God's one family.

How did Jesus break down barriers between God and the people? How does he unite all his followers in one family?

FOR US TODAY

1. God wants his people to live together in peace and fellowship. Jesus prayed for the unity of his people.

   Read John 17:20-23.
      Has Jesus' prayer been answered?
      Why are Christians divided into various denominations?
      How can we show that we all belong to the one family of God?

2. Why should all the members of a congregation be concerned about each other? Give examples of how love and care is being shown in your congregation.

WORSHIP

Dear Father,
You have made us all one in Christ:
   Help us to live in peace with each other.

You have brought us into your one family:
   Help us to be true friends to each other.

You have shown love and care for the whole world:
   Help us to love each other. For Jesus' sake. Amen.

Scripture references: Act 8:26-40; 9:1-30; 10; 11:1-26.

WITH YOUR FAMILY

Find pictures of people of various races. Paste the pictures around the caption: ALL ONE IN CHRIST. Display the illustrations in the room where your family eats together.

As a devotion, read the story of Philip and the Ethiopian in Acts 8:26-39, and talk about the unity we have with believers in Christ all around the world. Close with the Lord's Prayer.

MORE TO DO

1. Fill out your time-line. Scholars believe that Paul became a Christian in about AD 34, and began his first journey in AD 46.

2. Find Joppa, Samaria, and Antioch on a map to see how the Gospel was spreading.

3. Find out about the work of our church in a foreign country. As a class project, make posters of the work for Jesus in this country. Display your work in the church.

4. If people who have come from overseas belong to your congregation, ask them about the church in their home country. List the various countries from which people in your congregation have come.

5. Discuss ways in which we can witness for Jesus.

31

God builds his church

People have erected some magnificent buildings down through the centuries. But nobody has ever put up a building which could stand for ever.
Give examples of some old buildings which are now just ruins.

Jesus promised his disciples that God would build a Church which **would last for ever**. No one, not even the devil, would be able to destroy this Church.

Jesus did not mean a church made of stones or bricks, like Solomon's temple. God's Church would be made up of **people**. Jesus himself would be the 'foundation' of the Church, and Christians would be the 'living stones' built on this foundation.

BUILDERS FOR GOD

God used special 'builders' to carry out his plan. The men he sent out to build his Church were called 'apostles'. Most of them belonged to the band of 12 disciples who were with Jesus from the beginning, and had heard his teaching and seen his great works. The apostles were men who had seen Jesus risen from the dead.

The apostles built God's Church by telling people the Good News about Jesus. From Jerusalem they spread the story of Jesus further and further. By the time the apostles died, there were Christian congregations in most of the important cities of the Roman Empire, cared for by pastors, teachers and other leaders whom the apostles had trained.

PAUL — A MASTER BUILDER

The Apostle Paul was a key man in God's church-building program. On his missionary journeys, Paul preached the Gospel to all kinds of people —to Jews and Gentiles, to kings and soldiers, to idol-worshippers and to clever philosophers. 'I am not ashamed of the Gospel', he said. 'It is God's power to save all who believe.'

When visiting cities on his journeys, Paul usually preached the Gospel to the Jews first, telling them that Jesus was the promised Messiah. But many of the Jews rejected his preaching. He was saddened to see how the nation which had waited so long for the coming of the Messiah rejected the Saviour whom God had sent.

So Paul turned to the Gentiles. Wherever he went, God blessed his preaching so that new 'living stones' were built on to Jesus, the foundation of the Church. Paul kept in touch with these first Christians. Sometimes he revisited them on a later journey. To many of the congregations he wrote letters to encourage them and to strengthen them in their life as Christians.

Paul's work was not easy. He was often hunted, persecuted, and jailed by his enemies. But God gave him strength to continue. At the end of his life he could say: 'I have fought the good fight, I have finished the race, I have kept the faith' (2 Timothy 4:7).

PAUL'S MISSIONARY JOURNEYS
(Trace his journeys on the maps)

FIRST JOURNEY: Acts 13,14

Paul and Barnabas travelled through Cyprus and Asia Minor (Turkey), preaching in many places. Groups of believers were gathered in many towns.

For one of the exciting stories in this journey, read Acts 14:8–20

Why did the Jews become such bitter enemies of Paul?

How did God bless the work of Paul and Barnabas?

SECOND JOURNEY: Acts 15:40–18:22

With Silas as his helper, Paul travelled again through Asia Minor. An important new stage in his work came when he reached Troas. In Acts 16:6–10 we read how God led him into Europe. Paul travelled through Macedonia and Greece, and for the first time the Gospel was preached in Europe. Once again, God blessed the work so that many congregations were formed.

Read in Acts 16:19–30 about Paul and Silas in Philippi.

Talk about how the jailer became a believer.

THIRD JOURNEY: Acts 19 – 21:6

After a long stay in Ephesus, Paul travelled again through Macedonia and Greece, revisiting the congregations he had started. Then he returned to Jerusalem. Through the work of Paul and his helpers in important centres like Ephesus and Corinth, more and more people joined the church.

Read in Acts 19:8–20 about Paul's work in Ephesus.

How did Paul's work show the power of Jesus over Satan?

JOURNEY TO ROME

For some years Paul was kept in jail in Caesarea. But then he was sent as a prisoner to Rome. The Bible story about Paul's work ends with him in Rome, preaching the Gospel. Many believe Paul died in Rome during the persecution of Christians by Emperor Nero.

Read about how Paul was shipwrecked in Acts 27:13–44.

Why could Paul be sure of God's protection?

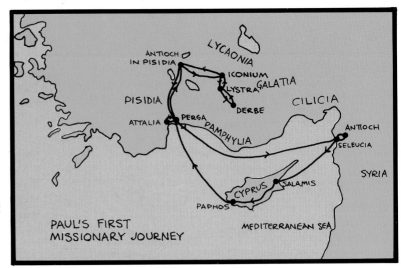

PAUL'S FIRST MISSIONARY JOURNEY

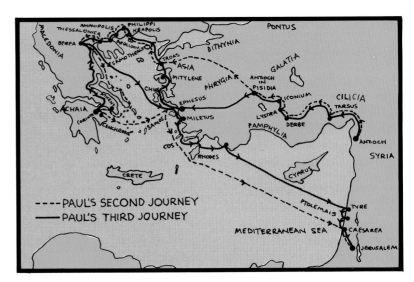

----- PAUL'S SECOND JOURNEY
——— PAUL'S THIRD JOURNEY

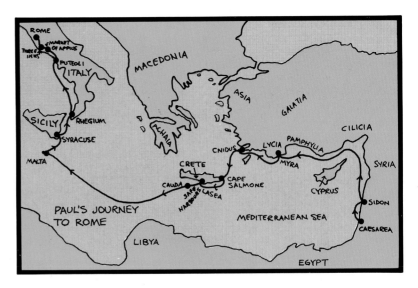

PAUL'S JOURNEY TO ROME

GOD WORKING THROUGH OTHER APOSTLES

All the apostles and their helpers were important in God's plans to build his Church. The New Testament does not tell us where the other apostles worked for Jesus after they left Jerusalem, although there are many old stories about them. Some of these stories tell us that Peter finally came to Rome and died there as a martyr; that John worked for many years in Ephesus. Some believe that Thomas went as far as India, and was killed as he preached the Gospel to the heathen people.

God used the apostles to write the books of the New Testament. Some of the apostles (Paul, James, Peter, and John) wrote letters (called Epistles) teaching more about God's plan to save the world through Jesus and to show Christians how to live as God's people. The evangelists (Matthew, Mark, Luke, and John) wrote the four Gospels, telling the story of Jesus which the apostles preached.

In the course of time, Christians gathered these writings of the apostles and evangelists to form the New Testament. These writings, together with the Old Testament, became the Christian Bible — the Word of God through which God carried on his plan to build his Church in the whole, wide world.

HERE ARE THE MAIN POINTS

- God used the apostles to build his Church.
  Through their work, God's Church kept on growing and expanding into many different lands.

- God's chosen people of the Old Testament — the Jews — generally rejected Jesus. But many Gentiles believed the Gospel and became members of the Christian Church, God's 'new Israel'.

- God inspired the apostles and their helpers to write the books of the New Testament. In the Bible we now have the true record of how God carried out his saving plan through Jesus.

KEY BIBLE PASSAGE   **EPHESIANS 2:19–22**

Christ is the strong foundation on which God built his Church.

How did God work through the apostles and prophets to lay this foundation?

GOD'S PEOPLE TODAY

1. God's Church today is built on the same foundation which the apostles laid.

   Read 1 Corinthians 3:10, 11.
   > How does God build his Church today?
   > What is the only foundation of God's Church?
   > Discuss why, in the Nicene Creed, we call the Christian Church 'apostolic'.

2. Jesus told his apostles to preach the Gospel to all nations. Today we see that the Gospel has spread throughout the world.

   Discuss ways in which the Gospel is spread in the world today.

WORSHIP

We sing thy praise, O God:
We own thee as our Lord.
All the earth doth worship thee:
Father from eternity.
The twelve apostles, one and all:
The holy prophets thou didst call.
The Church doth honour and proclaim:
Throughout the world thy holy name.
Holy is God, our Lord:
Holy is God, our Lord.
Holy is God, our Lord:
The Lord of Sabaoth.

INVOLVE YOUR FAMILY

Show your family these symbols of some of the apostles. Discuss their meaning.

Read Ephesians 2:19–22 for a family devotion, and use responsively the opening section of the *Te Deum* (printed at left) as a prayer of praise.

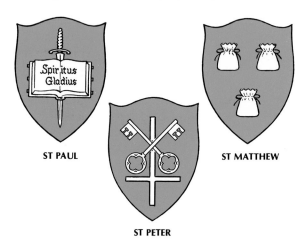

ST PAUL   ST MATTHEW

ST PETER

MORE TO DO

1. Read more about Paul on his journeys:
Paul in Thessalonica — Acts 17:1–9;
Paul in Corinth — Acts 18:1–17;
a plot against Paul — Acts 23:12–35.
2. Find out what Christian tradition tells us about the work and death of some of the apostles, such as Peter, John, Thomas, or Paul, and report this to the class. (Use a Bible dictionary or encyclopaedia to get the information.)
3. Read Acts 12:1–7 to find out how God set Peter free from prison.
4. God has used many people to help build his Church since the time of the apostles. Choose one of the following missionaries, famous in Christian history, find out something about him, and report back to the class: St Columba; St Boniface; William Carey; Hudson Taylor; Johannes Flierl.

Scripture references: Acts 13 – 28.

Waiting in hope

Mr and Mrs Smith were told that they could adopt Jimmy. Immediately they wrote to him: 'We are coming soon to take you home with us.' Jimmy wondered what his new home would be like.

How do you think he felt while he waited to go to his new home?
How would it help Jimmy if he knew that Mr and Mrs Smith were kind and loving?

LOOKING FORWARD TO GOING HOME

Before Jesus left his disciples, he told them: 'I am going to prepare a place for you. I will come back and take you to myself so that you will be where I am' (John 14:2,3).

This promise is the last great step in God's plan: to take his people home to live with Jesus for ever. Everything in that home will be perfect. There will be no sin, no suffering, no tears, no death. All who live with God in heaven will be perfectly happy for ever and ever.

With this promise, Jesus gave his followers something wonderful to look forward to. But he did not say when he would come to take them home. Until his return, he wanted them to work for him — to preach the Good News about God's love everywhere, so that God could gather in people of all nations to be his holy family.

SPREADING THE MESSAGE OF HOPE

The first Christians hoped Jesus would return in their own lifetime. But they had plenty to do while they waited for God to take the last great step in his plan. The apostles, and the Christians who lived after their time, kept on spreading the Gospel of Jesus to more and more countries. By about AD 320, the Roman Empire became Christian. In the centuries since then, the Church has been spreading to every country and every nation — just as God planned.

A FIERCE STRUGGLE

It has never been easy for God's people to carry on the work Jesus gave them to do. They have had to face opposition and suffering. Satan and his evil forces fight against God and his people. They try to stop the Gospel being spread, and to prevent people from coming into God's kingdom.

The last book of the Bible, the Revelation to John, tells us about this great struggle which has been going on ever since the time of Jesus, and which will continue until Jesus comes to take his people home. John describes the struggle in strange visions and symbols. But this book has wonderful comfort and hope for God's faithful people. Jesus will have the victory! Nothing can stop God carrying out everything according to his plan, and gathering in his people to live with him for ever.

BIBLE SEARCH
READ REVELATION 21:1-4; 22:1-5.

Why is heaven described as a beautiful city?
What will it be like in this heavenly city?
What will give God's people their greatest happiness (22:4)?

PERSECUTION

One way Satan fights against God and his plan is to turn other people against Christians. Already in the time of the apostles, Nero, a cruel Roman emperor, killed many people just because they were Christians. Later emperors also persecuted the followers of Jesus by throwing them into prison, torturing them, or cruelly putting them to death. Thousands of Christians died as faithful 'martyrs' (witnesses).

Still today, Christians in some parts of the world meet with hatred, violence, and even death, because they follow Jesus.

But this persecution has not destroyed God's Church or stopped the Gospel from spreading. In fact, the strong and brave faith of Christian martyrs has led many people to follow Jesus. Their example has also encouraged other Christians to hold fast to their faith.

FALSE TEACHING

Another way in which Satan has tried to destroy God's Church is by false teaching. There have been many people calling themselves teachers of God's Word who have taught their own ideas. Some Christians have lost their faith by believing these lies about God, about Jesus, about God's plan of salvation. False teaching has also caused quarrels and divisions among Christians.

But God has kept his promises. He has always given his people preachers and teachers who have taught his Word correctly and with great power. Down through the centuries, God has always kept a loyal group of true believers who have held fast to the Gospel.

FAITH AND LOVE GROWING COLD

Some of the most dangerous times for the Christian church are when everything seems to be going well for God's people. At such times, people are tempted to think they do not need God any more, and that they can manage all right by themselves.

God's Word continually encourages Christians to remain firm in their faith and to grow in their love for God. In the book of Revelation, Jesus says to his people: 'Be faithful to me, even if it means death, and I will give you life as your prize of victory' (Revelation 2:10).

BIBLE SEARCH
READ JOHN 11:20–27.

Death does not mean defeat for God's people. They know that when they die, they are safe in the hands of God. God uses even death to carry out his plan.

Why does death mean victory for believers in Christ?

Why can we be sure of eternal life?

ACCORDING TO PLAN

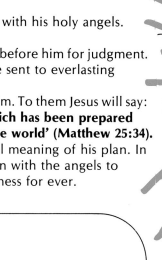

Through the whole history of this world, God has been carrying out his plan, and he will continue to do so to the very end of the world. Satan fights hard against God and his people — but he cannot win! Jesus won the victory over him when he rose from the dead. Now the Lord is with his people in all their trouble. They live in the sure hope of final victory when Jesus comes to take his people home.

On the last day, Jesus will come in glory with his holy angels.

- All the dead will be raised to life.
- All who have ever lived will be gathered before him for judgment.
- Those who do not believe in him will be sent to everlasting punishment.
- His faithful followers will rejoice to see him. To them Jesus will say:

'Come and possess the kingdom which has been prepared for you ever since the creation of the world' (Matthew 25:34).

Then, at last, God will make plain the full meaning of his plan. In their heavenly home, God's people will join with the angels to praise God and serve him in perfect happiness for ever.

BIBLE SEARCH
READ REVELATION 7:9–17.
Why do God's people celebrate in heaven?
Why can we be sure we will share in this celebration?

are included in God's plan. You can be sure that everything is still going according to his plan. God is in control as your loving and almighty Father.

As you wait for God to complete his plan for you, you can join in the prayer of God's people:

AMEN! COME, LORD JESUS!
THIS IS MOST CERTAINLY TRUE!

KEY BIBLE PASSAGE   TITUS 2:11–14

What kind of lives will God help us to lead as we wait for Jesus to come?

Talk about God's final plan for his people.

Write down some of the things you have learnt from studying God's plan. Share these thoughts with your family.

As a devotion, read the section 'According to Plan' above, followed by 1 Peter 1:6–11. Read a suitable hymn as the prayer.

FOR DISCUSSION

1. Review Lessons 17–31 and discuss what the various stories tell us about God's plans.

2. Give examples of how we have to struggle against evil as we try to live as God's people.

Read 1 Peter 1:6–11.
> How does God use trials to help us be faithful?
> What will be the final result for us, according to God's plan?

3. Choose a hymn or a song which speaks about our Christian hope. Read it, and discuss what it says.

MORE TO DO

1. Review Lessons 17–31. To help you do this, each member of the class could work out a quiz on one or more chapters for testing out the class.

2. You are included in God's plan! Share with the class how this makes you feel. Tell how this course has helped you as one of God's people.

3. Read 1 Thessalonians 5:1–8. What is Paul's advice to Christians as they wait for Jesus to come?

4. Find out how the following teachers tried to mislead the church: Arius; Joseph Smith; Ellen G. White; C.T. Russell. How can we be on our guard against all false teachers?

5. Many famous Christian martyrs have died confessing their faith in Jesus. Find out about one of these, and report back to the class.

WORSHIP

Join in the praise of the saints in heaven (Revelation 15:3,4):

Lord God Almighty, how great and wonderful are
  your deeds!
King of the nations, how right and true are your ways!
Who will not fear you, Lord? Who will refuse to declare
  your greatness?
You alone are holy. All the nations will come and
  worship you,
Because your just actions are seen by all.

Scripture references: The Revelation.

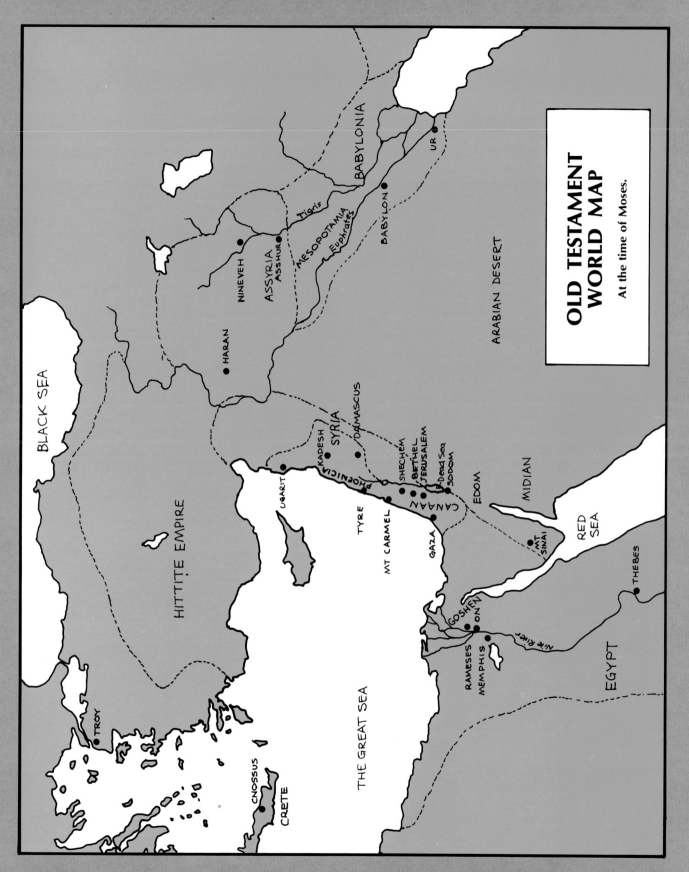

**OLD TESTAMENT
WORLD MAP**

At the time of Moses.

BLACK SEA

BABYLONIA

UR

Tigris

MESOPOTAMIA

Euphrates

NINEVEH

ASSYRIA
ASSHUR

BABYLON

ARABIAN DESERT

HARAN

HITTITE EMPIRE

DAMASCUS

KADESH

SYRIA

SHECHEM
BETHEL
JERUSALEM

Dead Sea
SODOM

UGARIT

PHOENICIA

TYRE

MT CARMEL

CANAAN

GAZA

EDOM

MIDIAN

MT
SINAI

RED
SEA

THEBES

TROY

GOSHEN
ON

RAMESES
MEMPHIS

Nile River

EGYPT

THE GREAT SEA

CNOSSUS

CRETE

ACCORDING TO PLAN
TIME LINE OF OLD AND NEW TESTAMENT

This time-line sets out God's plan from the beginning to the end of time. Jesus is the centre of world history, according to God's plan.

Main events and people are pictured by symbols, which are also included in the lesson material. Check where each lesson symbol belongs on the time-line so that you can pinpoint its place in the history of God's plan.

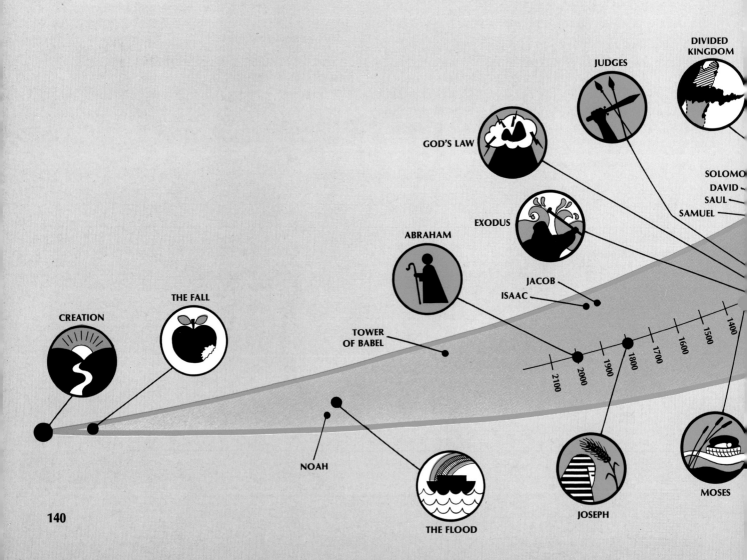

CREATION

THE FALL

NOAH

THE FLOOD

TOWER OF BABEL

ABRAHAM

ISAAC

JACOB

JOSEPH

MOSES

EXODUS

GOD'S LAW

JUDGES

DIVIDED KINGDOM

SOLOMON

DAVID

SAUL

SAMUEL

2100 2000 1900 1800 1700 1600 1500 1400

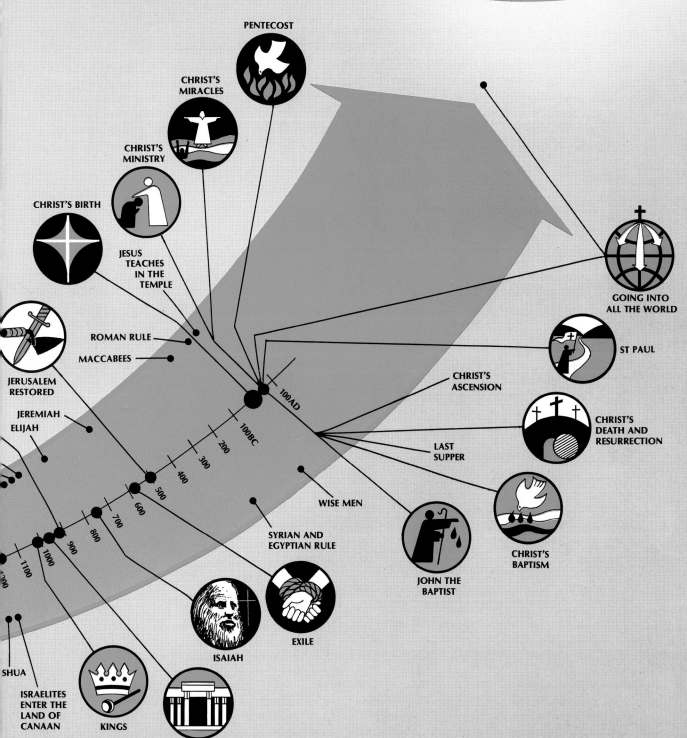

PENTECOST

CHRIST'S
MIRACLES

CHRIST'S
MINISTRY

CHRIST'S BIRTH

JESUS
TEACHES
IN THE
TEMPLE

ROMAN RULE

MACCABEES

JERUSALEM
RESTORED

JEREMIAH
ELIJAH

100AD

100BC

200

300

400

500

600

700

800

900

1000

1100

200

GOING INTO
ALL THE WORLD

ST PAUL

CHRIST'S
ASCENSION

CHRIST'S
DEATH AND
RESURRECTION

LAST
SUPPER

WISE MEN

CHRIST'S
BAPTISM

SYRIAN AND
EGYPTIAN RULE

JOHN THE
BAPTIST

SHUA

ISRAELITES
ENTER THE
LAND OF
CANAAN

KINGS

TEMPLE

ISAIAH

EXILE

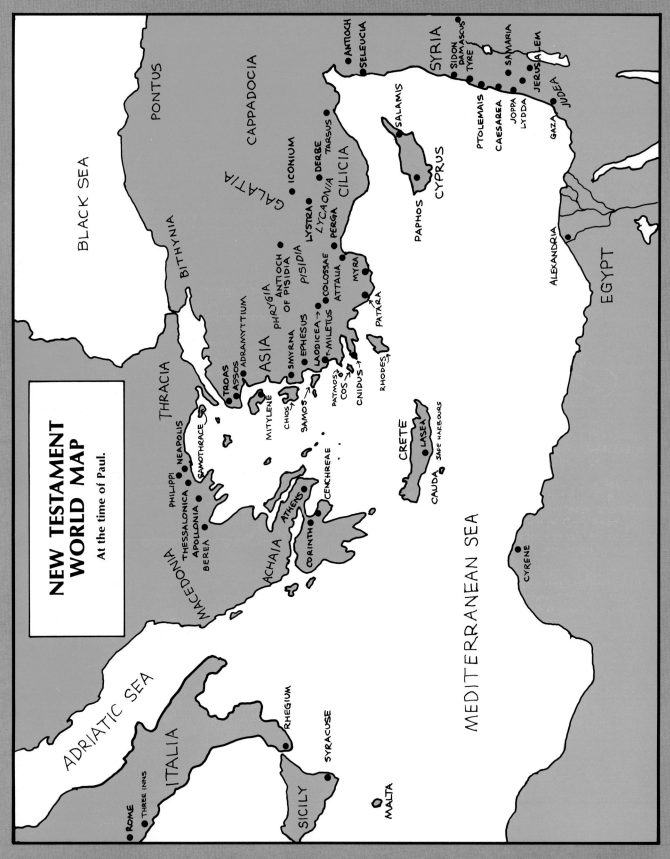

NEW TESTAMENT WORLD MAP

At the time of Paul.

BLACK SEA

PONTUS

CAPPADOCIA

SYRIA

ANTIOCH
SELEUCIA

SIDON
DAMASCUS
TYRE

SAMARIA

JERUSALEM

PTOLEMAIS
CAESAREA
JOPPA
LYDDA
JUDEA
GAZA

SALAMIS

CYPRUS

PAPHOS

GALATIA

BITHYNIA

ICONIUM

DERBE
LYSTRA
LYCAONIA
PERGA
TARSUS
CILICIA

ATTALIA

MYRA

PATARA

RHODES

ALEXANDRIA

EGYPT

THRACIA

ASIA

PHRYGIA

ANTIOCH
OF PISIDIA

PISIDIA

COLOSSAE

LAODICEA
MILETUS
EPHESUS
SMYRNA
ADRAMYTTIUM
ASSOS
TROAS

MITYLENE

CHIOS

SAMOS

PATMOS
COS
CNIDUS

SAMOTHRACE

NEAPOLIS

PHILIPPI

THESSALONICA
APOLLONIA
BEREA

MACEDONIA

ACHAIA

ATHENS

CORINTH

CENCHREAE

CRETE

LASEA

SAFE HARBOURS

CAUDA

MEDITERRANEAN SEA

CYRENE

ADRIATIC SEA

ITALIA

RHEGIUM

SYRACUSE

SICILY

MALTA

ROME
THREE INNS

142

INDEX

(listing the main references to biblical names, events, and topics)